THE MAN IN THE ARENA

THE CALL TO END TIME LEADERSHIP

DR. CHRISTOPHER MARK D'AMICO

Published by:
RH Publishing
Dallas, TX. 75240
www.rhpublishingcompany.com

Copyright © 2024, Dr. Christopher Mark D'Amico

ISBN#978-1-960494-06-1

All rights reserved under International Copyright Law. Written permission must be secured from the publisher/author to reproduce, copy, or transmit any part of this book, regardless of the format.

Unless otherwise noted, all scripture quotations are taken from the King James Version of the Bible.

Scriptures marked AMP are taken from the AMPLIFIED BIBLE (AMP): Scripture taken from the AMPLIFIED® BIBLE, Copyright © 1954, 1958, 1962, 1964, 1965, 1987 by the Lockman Foundation Used by Permission. (www.Lockman.org)

Scriptures marked TLB are taken from THE LIVING BIBLE (TLB): Scripture taken from THE LIVING BIBLE copyright© 1971. Used by permission of Tyndale House Publishers, Inc., Carol Stream, Illinois 60188. All rights reserved.

Scriptures marked TM are taken from THE MESSAGE: THE BIBLE IN CONTEMPORARY ENGLISH (TM): Scripture taken from THE MESSAGE: THE BIBLE IN CONTEMPORARY ENGLISH, copyright©1993, 1994, 1995, 1996, 2000, 2001, 2002. Used by permission of NavPress Publishing Group.

ENDORSEMENTS

What A book! Filled with revelation knowledge, that every believer needs to read. A must for developing leaders, as well as equipping the body of Christ, honoring and protecting God-set leadership. This is a God send for this hour. Thank you, Dr. Chris, for your ministry of excellence to the Body of Christ.

Pastor Peter Doseck
Only Believe Church
Botkins, Ohio

Dr. Chris D'Amico, in his new book on Leadership, will bless you. He is a strong leader who is contending for the faith and supernatural! God is raising up Leaders who will not compromise His Word and are not ashamed of the Holy Spirit. It will take a whole new wave of godly leaders to be raised up to see America shaken by the power of the Holy Spirit.

    I pray, as you read this book, you will be stirred up. It's time for you to rise up and take your place.

Dr. Rodney Howard-Browne
Senior Pastor/Founder of the River at Tampa Bay Church
River University
Tampa, Florida

Dr. Chris D'Amico is an anointed, biblically versed evangelist, who moves in the prophetic realm spiritually and clearly understands leadership. Follow his lead, and read the book!

Evangelist Darryl Strawberry
4 Times World Series Champion
St. Charles County, Missouri

First of all, I would like to say that Dr. Chris D'Amico is my friend, and I have known him and his faithful walk for many years. He is a prophetic teacher whose life, ministry and giftings are Word centered, and he lives a lifestyle accordingly. He is a man who places high value to honor culture and loyalty in friendships. He always knows to fight his situations through the Word of God, coming forth victorious, as an overcomer. He has an immense experience in walking with the Lord and walking in the Word. He is an amazing prophet and a powerful leader of our time.

I've had the blessing of hosting him in my church and was so blessed to see the way the Word flows out of him, and it is confirmed by the signs and wonders, which will not be forgotten by our church members.

In this book, Dr. Chris will take you on a journey of how to have a solid relationship with God, and developing integrity that will lead you to divine places in your lives and calling. You will evolve, knowing that Jesus is your safe place and fortress.

I pray that everyone who reads this book will receive a similar addiction that he has for the Word and prayer. So, read this book! Read it again and again. Experience it, and teach this, and see your personal faith as well as the faith of others increase.

Apostle Dr. Rambo
Founder and President Rambo World Outreach
Bengelore, India

One of the greatest needs of the church today is leadership. In this book, Dr. Chris gives us a revelation in the Word of God that divinely approves leadership. In today's church we need leaders that contend for the glory of God. Dr. Chris has done an excellent job at preparing leaders for this generation.

Reverend Mark Hankins
Mark Hankins Ministries
Alexandria, Louisiana

Dr. Chris D'Amico is a personal friend and brother in Christ to me. He is a man of high ministerial ethics and integrity, as well as a strong leader in the Body of Christ.

His book on leadership contains a wealth of vital and key information in a very timely manner.

I strongly recommend this book and know it will be a great blessing to leaders and all who aspire to leadership!

J.D. Hill
Catch The Vision Ministries
NFL Professional Football Player—The Buffalo Bills, Detroit Lions
Phoenix Dream Center
Chandler, Arizona

Dr. Chris D'Amico has written a very unique book on leadership. I always like to point out to every Christian that you can only go higher if you have a solid foundation.

Instead of laying out a formula of specific leadership skills, Dr. D'Amico helps every leader with an established, very biblical, spiritual foundation on which to build a solid life and ministry that cannot be shaken. I appreciate his approach because it is so similar to what we endeavor to do for our students at LCU. We have a course entitled "Christlike Character" because I have long believed that a person's gifts and talents may get them on the platform of ministry, but the only thing that will keep them there is the integrity and moral strength that comes only through Christ's power by the Holy Spirit.

Dr. D'Amico covers the most vital topics of this necessary foundation, with great scriptural underpinnings and truly inspiring quotes from some of the greatest leaders known to man. I especially appreciate his treatment of the essentials for those who are called alongside to partner in assisting a leader though a right heart attitude. This will not only bring great success to any gospel endeavor, such as establishing a powerful church, or a successful evangelistic outreach, but will also bring glory and honor to our Savior and Lord, King Jesus.

Your life will be blessed by reading this book diligently, and applying it to your leadership foundation.

Congratulations should be given to Dr. Chris D'Amico for a job well done in authoring such an essential and timely book.

Dr. Doug Wingate
President and Founder, Life Christian University
Tampa, Florida

Dr. Chris D'Amico is an anointed biblically versed evangelist, who moves in the prophetic realm and knows leadership.

He has spoken into my life in many ways, personally and professionally, as I make video productions, and I truly treasure his friendship.

I think this book will be of great impact to you, because he knows how to lead people, he is and intuitive leader himself, and he brilliantly explains the biblical steps, mind-set, and heart attitude to make an impact in people's lives.

Dr. Chris is all about impacting people, and leading them to realize the best God has for them. I so appreciate him as my friend, and I so appreciate this book. You should read it, because it will have a tremendous impact on you and bless you greatly.

Dr. Stephen Yake
Producer/Writer Yake Films
Sarasota, Florida

One of the focal points of *The Call to End Time Leadership* is the need for leaders to train leaders, and not merely followers. Paul trained Timothy, who trained faithful men, who trained others. We are all followers of Christ, yet servant-leaders. Dr. Chris recognizes the importance for leaders to not only lead followers, but to lead leaders. Paul wasn't afraid to be succeeded. He always focused on the strengths of people.

The Man in the Arena is a teacher, soldier, athlete, banker, coach, vessel and servant. A great team consists of a diverse reservoir of talent. Yet Dr. Chris reminds us that gifts and talent are only potential if it's without submission to the Lord Jesus Christ. As we move forward in the 21st Century, this book is not only a must read, but it's a divine and timely revelation for the church to continue to lift up a Light in a dark world.

Joe Jackson
Evangelist—Associate Pastor, Full Life Church,
Chandler, Arizona
New York Jets, Minnesota Vikings DE

THE MAN IN THE ARENA

"It is not the critic who counts; not the man who points out how the strong man stumbles or where the doer of deeds could have done better. The credit belongs to the man who is actually in the arena, whose face is marred by dust and sweat and blood, who strives valiantly, who errs, who comes short again and again. Because there is no effort without error and shortcoming, but who does actually strive to do the deeds, who knows great enthusiasms, the great devotions, who spends himself in a worthy cause, who at the best knows in the end the triumph of high achievement, and who at the worst, if he fails, at least fails while DARING GREATLY, so that his place shall never be with those cold and timid souls who neither know victory nor defeat."

THEODORE ROOSEVELT
October 27, 1858 - January 6, 1919
26th President of the U.S. 1901-1909

A CALL TO LEADERSHIP

"All of the great leaders have had one characteristic in common: it was the willingness to confront unequivocally the major anxiety of their people in their time. This, and not much else, is the essence of leadership."
—John Kenneth Galbraith

"The price of greatness is responsibility." —Winston Churchill

"Leaders aren't born, they are made. And they are made just like anything else, through hard work. And that's the price we'll have to pay to achieve that goal, or any goal." —Vince Lombardi

"Most of the important things in the world have been accomplished by people who have kept on trying when there seemed to be no hope at all."
—Dale Carnegie

"A true leader has the confidence to stand alone, the courage to make tough decisions, and the compassion to listen to the needs of others. He does not set out to be a leader, but becomes one by the equality of his actions and the integrity of his intent." —Douglas MacArthur

"Success is not final, failure is not fatal: it is the courage to continue that counts." —Winston Churchill

"You gain strength, courage and confidence in which you really stop to look fear in the face. You must do the thing you think you cannot do."
—Eleanor Roosevelt

"Successful leaders see the opportunities in every difficulty rather than the difficulty in every opportunity." —Reed Markham

"The greatest leader is not necessarily the one who does the greatest things. He is the one that gets the people to do the greatest things."
—Ronald Reagan

"Treat people as if they were what they ought to be, and you help them become what they are capable of being." —Johann Wolfgang von Goethe

"If your actions inspire others to dream more, learn more, do more, and become more, you are a leader." —John Quincy Adams

"Leadership is the art of getting someone else to do something you want done because he wants to do it." —Dwight D. Eisenhower

"Leadership is lifting a person's vision to high sights, the raising of a person's performance to a higher standard, the building of a personality beyond its normal limitations." —Peter F. Drucker

"Leadership is the capacity to translate vision into reality."
—Warren G. Bennis

"Nearly all men can stand adversity, but if you want to test a man's character, give him power." —Abraham Lincoln

"The quality of a leader is reflected in the standards they set for themselves." —Ray Kroc

"The supreme quality of leadership is integrity." —Dwight D. Eisenhower

"No man will make a great leader who wants to do it all himself, or to get all the credit for doing it." —Andrew Carnegie

"Outstanding leaders go out of the way to boost the self-esteem of their personnel. If people believe in themselves, it's amazing what they can accomplish." —Sam Walton

"Effective leadership is not about making speeches or being liked; leadership is defined by results not attributes." —Peter Drucker

"Whatever you are, be a good one." —Abraham Lincoln

TABLE OF CONTENTS

INTRODUCTION 13

Chapter 1
RELATIONSHIP OVER RELIGION 19

Chapter 2
WALKING IN DIVINE LOVE 31

Chapter 3
SPIRITUAL HUNGER 37

Chapter 4
INTEGRITY—THE SURE FOUNDATION FOR SUCCESS 47

Chapter 5
FAITHFULNESS—GOD'S PROVING GROUND
FOR PROMOTION 57

Chapter 6
DIVINELY DESIGNED TO HAVE DOMINION 71

Chapter 7
HEARING THE VOICE OF GOD 77

Chapter 8
THE PLACE OF ABIDING 85

Chapter 9
WEATHERING THE STORMS WITHOUT BEING
WEATHERED 93

Chapter 10
OVERCOMING SETBACKS 101

Chapter 11
PROPER ATTITUDES TOWARD GODLY LEADERSHIP 117

Chapter 12 127
LIFTING THE HANDS OF GODLY LEADERS

Chapter 13 133
CONTENDING FOR HIS PRESENCE

INTRODUCTION

I was raised a good, Catholic boy in Lewiston, New York, the youngest of four boys. My parents always did their best to establish in our home the need for God and a respect for the things of God. My father was a pharmacist and a successful businessman, owning—with five other partners—three multi-purpose stores, with pharmacies inside them. Looking back, they were ahead of their time, on a smaller scale embracing the concept of a modern-day Walmart. You might say our family was living the American dream.

On my father's side of the family, my grandmother, who died before I was born, was a Catholic nun. She later desired to be married, and left her nun hood to marry my grandfather. They had two children, my father and his sister, my aunt. I make mention of this because our family roots held a great deal of respect for God and living an honorable, moral life. I never want to leave the impression that those involved with religious organizations, have not had personal experiences with God, because they have. All I know is, I had a concept of God, but I really did not know Him.

LEAVING TRADITION

I believe that all religious institutions mean well, but unless it comes down to a personal relationship with Jesus Christ, it holds no transforming power. 2 Timothy 3:5 declares, there will be those in the last days mesmerized with a religion form, but having no real evidence of power. ***"Having a form of godliness, but denying the power thereof: from such turn away."*** The Phillips Translation declares, ***"They will maintain a façade of religion."*** The Taylor's Translation declares, ***"They will go to church, yes ..."***

I have said it for years, ***"going to church, doesn't make you a Christian any more than sitting in a garage will make you a car."*** There are enormous thousands of individuals, all over the United States and the world, that attend some sort of religious service, but there is no transforming power from the Holy Spirit of God. It is only the manifested presence of God Almighty working in our midst that separates religious tradition from a true and living relationship with God.

The Basic English Translation declares, *"… They will turn their backs on the power."* I have talked with many religious skeptics through my countless years of ministry and serving God, who basically have reasoned away the authenticity of the gospel and have missed God. They have made themselves strangers to the power of God, turning their back on the very thing they need the most. The devil has done a good job of selling to the world, you can continue attending a weekly religious service, and live the other six days of the week as a sinner and still make heaven. The message Bible, of 2 Timothy 3:5, is very direct, *"They'll make a show of religion, but behind the scenes they're animals."*

This is true in our country from the government, military, Wall Street and cooperate world. They speak of God as though they know Him, even using His name to make a show of religion, but behind the scenes, they live contradicting lifestyles that are contrary to the transforming power of the living God. I am not suggesting this is true of all those listed above, because God has countless men and women in all sects of society that honor Him as true Christians, bearing the fruit of His name. It's not the attending of a religious service, or paying a religious obligation that makes a man or women right with God, *but receiving Christ Jesus as Savior and living for Him. It is only having a living relationship with Him that will constitute reality.*

In 1 John 5:11-12, it declares, *"And this is the record, that God has given to us eternal life, and this life is in his Son. He that hath the Son hath life; and he that hath not the Son of God hath not life."* The Wade Translation declares, *"God has given to us eternal life, and it is in His Son that this life is to be found. He who possesses the Son, possesses this life. He who does not possess the Son does not possess this life."* Becoming a Christian means we are now possessors of the very life and substance of God himself. His presence comes to live on the inside, transforming the spirit of man into His image and likeness. In John 10:10, Jesus said, *"The thief cometh not, but for to steal, and to kill, and to destroy: I am come that you might have LIFE and have it MORE ANUNDANTLY."*

RELATIONSHIP OVER TRADITION

"There is no more urgent and critical question in life than that of your personal relationship with God and your eternal salvation."
—Billy Graham

I believe that God is looking for a *personal relationship* with man to transform our hearts first and foremost. Being raised in a traditional Italian home had many great experiences, from the extravagant pasta meals to the special holiday celebrations with all our relatives; we had a great time. Some traditions are wonderful and should be embraced and celebrated as your heritage. There are other traditions that are not so good to embrace, especially those that keep you from knowing God. Jesus said in Matthew 15:6b, *"… thus have ye made the commandment of God of none effect by your tradition."* The Goodspeed Translation reads, *"So you have nullified what God has said, for the sake of what has been HANDED DOWN TO YOU."*

When religious tradition nullifies what the truth of God's Word declares, we had better re-evaluate what has been handed down to embrace the real truth. In John 8:32, Jesus said, *"And ye shall KNOW THE TRUTH and the truth shall MAKE YOU FREE."* The Twentieth Century Translation declares, *"And you shall FIND OUT the truth and the truth shall MAKE YOU FREE."* It can be a shocking reality to awaken to the fact that something you may have believed all your life—ideas and concepts handed down—called tradition, is not really found in the Word of God. In John 17:17, Jesus define what truth is, *"Sanctify them through thy truth: THY WORD IS TRUTH."*

If God's Word is our standard to judge between tradition and reality, then we must find our answers from the scriptures found in the Bible. If you cannot find it in the Word of God, chapter and verse, then it's a form of deception and tradition. Religious tradition keeps us from freedom, while knowing the truth opens the doorway in our thinking to actually live free.

TRANSFORMING THE HEART

In Ezekiel 36:25-27, we get a snapshot from the scriptures, what God intended to do through the plan of redemption in Christ Jesus, ***"Then I will sprinkle clean water on you, and ye shall be clean: from all your filthiness, and from all your idols, will I cleanse you. A NEW HEART also will I give you, and a NEW SPIRIT WILL I PUT WITHIN YOU: and I will take away the stony heart out of your flesh, and give you an heart of flesh. And I will PUT MY SPIRIT WITHIN YOU and cause you to walk in my statues, and ye shall keep my judgements, and do them."***

During my high school years, I was exposed to a new form of religion, so I thought. There was an evangelistic ministry in Niagara Falls, New York, called the "Light house." I would have never been exposed to this except for the unusual changes that I witnessed in the lives of my two older brothers. They both had been good brothers; yet, like a lot of good young adults today, they had been involved in the party lifestyle that the world offers.

I still so vividly remember, as a young boy, working at my father's drug store. We were riding home one night in the car. We came to a stop sign close to our house, and my father broke down with emotional tears over the direction my two older brothers had gone. I remember him saying to me, "I am not sure where I have gone wrong in raising your brothers for them to be living the lifestyle that they have." His heart was so burdened that it left a lasting effect on me, even until today. The problem wasn't necessarily the lack of good upbringing or training by Dad or Mom, but that they were lost in sin nature, and needed their hearts to be transformed. Romans 3:23, declares, *"All have sinned and have fallen short of the glory of God."* The Barclay Translation declares, *"All have sinned; all have lost the divine glory which they were meant to have."*

It wasn't long after this encounter that my two older brothers came to have an encounter with their Heavenly Father. Both of them at separate times, not far apart, had come to the saving knowledge of Jesus Christ. As a result, they *changed dramatically*. God had washed away their filthiness and cleansed them of their sin nature, placing His Holy Spirit in their hearts. Both were set free from addictive behaviors.

"Therefore, if any man be in Christ, he is a new creature: old things are passed away; behold and all things are become new"
(2 Corinthians 5:17).

Today, amazingly enough, both are *ordained ministers of the Gospel!* It wasn't long before our entire family—father, mother, third oldest brother and me—all came to receive the free gift of eternal life. I still remember October 18, 1980, when I cried out to God for forgiveness of sins and Jesus Christ came into my heart. I have never been the same!

Chapter 1

RELATIONSHIP OVER RELIGION

"Go ye into all the world and preach the gospel to every creature. He that believeth and is baptized SHALL BE SAVED, but he that BELIEVETH NOT SHALL BE DAMNED"
(Mark 16:15-16).

"Life is a school room with glorious opportunity to prepare for eternity." —Billy Graham

"Heaven is real, and hell is real, and eternity is one breath away."
—Billy Graham

The fact remains—man is a sinner, separated from God, and needs a Savior. This is the reason the Gospel must be preached to all men, every nation and every tribe around the world. Jesus gave the Church the great commission when He said, **"GO INTO ALL THE WORLD ..."** What a sobering message to digest. Men either accept or believe, being given eternal life or they do not, to face the eternal judgment of hell. This is serious business.

Every week in our world, it is estimated that over two million people die and enter into eternity. We are living in a world, facing a new crisis called terrorism. Radical Muslim terrorists are willing to commit violent suicidal acts, not only killing themselves, but also killing many innocent lives. Those who have fallen victim, have been instantly ushered into eternity to face their fate.

Why is it that human nature is so calloused to these facts? The main reason, I believe, is our perspective has been living void of what the Bible declares. The common attitude of our culture is, "live for today and do whatever feels good." The only problem with that attitude is that it holds no fear of God. Proverbs 14:27, declares, **"The FEAR OF THE LORD is a fountain of life, to DEPART FROM THE SNARES OF DEATH."**

The Amplified Bible declares, *"Reverent and worshipful fear of the Lord is a fountain of life, that one may avoid the snares of death."*

Have you ever drawn the correlation between the fear of the Lord and long life? One very visible illustration can be seen in the lives of the Hollywood celebrities of the past. They experience fame, fortune and along with that a lot of reckless living. The reality is such that whether you are a Christian or not, the law of sin and death is out to destroy you. This is what the scripture calls, "the snare of death." Romans 8:2, declares, *"For the law of the Spirit of life in Christ Jesus hath made me free from the law of sin and death."* To make it simple, if you choose certain behaviors contrary to the laws of God, and persist in recklessly practicing them, you will eventually end up shipwrecked. The law of sin and death is real, and anyone choosing to sow into that law will reap the consequences of heartache and destruction. Proverbs 10:27, declares, *"The fear of the Lord prolongeth days: but the years of the wicked shall be shortened."*

The question is, how do we make the transition from hell to heaven, form sin to forgiveness, from bondage to freedom, from foolishness to wisdom? Only by honoring the Lord with our lives. Romans 10:9-10, tells us, *"That if thou shall confess with thy mouth the lord Jesus, and shalt believe in thine heart that God raised him from the dead, thou shalt be saved. For with the heart man believeth unto righteousness; and with the mouth confession is made unto salvation."* It's receiving Jesus Christ as Lord and looking to follow His Word as a guidepost for our decision making at all of life's crossroads that keeps us from the many snares of the laws of death, giving us long life. (Psalm 91:16).

GETTING ON THE RIGHT ROAD

The only peaceable solution for our lives is to get on the right road in life. We must live our lives *God's way* and *not ours*. In John 14:6, Jesus declared, *"I am the WAY, TRUTH and the LIFE, NO MAN COMES TO THE FATHER EXCEPT THROUGH ME."* The Philips Translation declares, *"I am The road ..."* The reality is such that if you have not received Jesus Christ as your personal Savior, you're on the wrong road. What road are we talking about? That would be the road that eventually leads to the eternal separation from God and hell. Proverbs 14:12 declares, ***"There is a way that seems right unto a man, but the end thereof are the ways of death."*** The Septuagint Translation makes it very clear, ***"There is a way which seemeth right to a man; but the end of it is at the bottom of hades."***

Religion cannot get you off that road. Science, government, or any other philosophy of the day, cannot get you off that road. Only Jesus can get you on the right road! Acts 4:12, declares, ***"Neither is there salvation in any other: for there is none other name under heaven given among men, whereby we must be saved."***

HELL'S ROAD OF DESTRUCTION

I will not take the time now to go into an in-depth study about hell, but we will say a few things on the subject before we go any farther. Most preachers and modern religion want to stay off the subject of hell, but we must alert and warn all not to go there. Generations of men and women have missed God and have found eternity in hell, being tormented. Whether the world today refuses to believe hell is a real place or not, doesn't change the reality of its existence. Proverbs 27:20, declares, ***"Hell and destruction are never full; so the eyes of man are never satisfied."*** The Message Bible speaks clearly of hell's intention toward mankind, ***"Hell has a veracious appetite, and lust just never quits."***

In Matthew 7:13, Jesus declares, ***"Wide is the gate, and broad is the way to destruction."*** Hell, obviously has an *entrance gate,* and there is plenty of room on that road for an individual who wants to go there. The Twentieth Century Translation declares, ***"Broad and spacious is the road."*** The Phillips Translation declares, ***"… and there are many people going that way."*** One well-known minister always said, ***"There is always a hell to shun and a heaven to gain."***

Mankind without a Savior is on the wrong road. The only way to say "No" to hell, is to say "YES" to heaven. Psalm 9:17 declares, ***"The wicked shall be turned into hell, all the nations that forget God."*** Heaven has a narrow gate, and that is only found and accessible through Jesus Christ. Matthew 7:14 declares, ***"Because strait is the gate, and NARROW is the WAY, which leads to LIFE."*** In John 6:35, Jesus declared, *"I am the bread of life: he that cometh to me shall never hunger; and he that believeth on me shall never thirst."* Jesus is that narrow gateway to eternal life!

John Chrysostom once said on the subject of hell, *"The 'pains of hell' are not the greatest part of hell. The 'loss of heaven' is really the weightiest woe of hell."* Billy Graham said, *"Some people will never understand the seriousness of eternity, until they step out into it unprepared."* He also said, *"The way we view death will determine the way we live our lives."* Winston Churchill, one of the greatest leaders in the history of England, said, *"You can trace the downfall of England when the preachers stopped preaching about hell."*

In Luke 9:25, Jesus said, *"For what is a man advantaged, if he gain the whole world, and lose himself or be a cast away?"* The New English Bible declares, *"What will a man gain by winning the whole world at the cost of his true self."* The Contemporary English Translation declares, *"What will you gain, if you own the whole world but destroy yourself or waste your life?"* If our life on this earth is short compared to eternity, then I think we should strongly consider the realities of the afterlife as very important. James 4:14, declares, *"Whereas ye know not what shall be on the morrow. For what is your life? It is a vapour, that appeareth for a little time, and the vanishes away."*

Dr. Lester Sumrall once said, *"The graveyard has two voices; I've been where you are at and you're coming to where I am at."* There is no way to avoid death at the end of one's life. Death is a doorway unto the eternal world, and we all will walk through that door for ourselves. Hebrews 9:27, declares, *"It is appointed unto men once to die, but after this the judgment seat."* The Message Bible declares, *"Everyone has to die once, then face the consequences."* The Isaacs Translation declares, *"And in so far as it is reserved to man once to die and after death to undergo that sifting which shall separate the evil from the good."*

At the doorway of death, all men and women will face the consequences of the choices they made in their lifetime. They will either be ushered by the angels into heaven or ushered by demons into hell. It seems to me, the choice is obvious, choose life! Deuteronomy 30:19, declares, *"I call heaven and earth to record this day against you, I have SET BEFORE YOU life and death, blessing and cursing: THEREFORE, CHOOSE LIFE, that both thou and thy seed may live."*

THE REDEMPTION OF MAN

When Christ came to redeem mankind, He redeemed him from a fallen state into a new creation. He didn't just come to spruce us up a bit. He came to completely remake man on the inside. The end result of the death, burial and resurrection of Jesus was a new race of men and women—called the new creation. 2 Corinthians 5:17, declares, ***"Therefore IF ANY MAN BE IN CHRIST, HE IS A NEW CREATION: old things are passed away; behold, all things are become new."*** Jesus came to annihilate sin within the redeemed and open up heaven as our home. What an amazing reality, our sins are forgiven and our nature has changed. What a blessing that old things, old ways, old habits, the old nature of sin has passed away. When Christ enters into our hearts, He comes to make everything new. Let's take a look at some different translations:

"Therefore, if any one be in union with Christ, he is a new being …" (TCNT)

" For if a man is in Christ, he becomes a new person altogether …" (Phillips Translation)

"Therefore, if a man is a Christian, he is a brand new creation. The old guy is gone, a new man has appeared." (Cotton Patch Translation)

"A true Christian is not merely a man altered, but a man remade." (Doaf Translation)

"When a man becomes a Christian, he becomes brand new person inside. He is not the same anymore. A new life has begun." (The Living Bible)

THE REMADE MAN

One author articulated the new birth like this, ***"Down through the ages of human history, every step, every dealing with man has been toward one goal, a new creation man."*** The new creation, would produce a caliber of men and women with a new spiritual condition, completely free from spiritual death and satanic dominion. Jesus declared, *"Unless a person is born again (a new from above), he cannot ever see (know, be acquainted with, and experience) the kingdom of God."* (John 3:3, AMP). The miracle of the new birth goes into action the moment someone accepts Christ as Savior. The sin nature is driven out and the very life and nature of God enters within. A man or women receiving Christ as Lord, becomes re-fathering from above. The new birth means we are born into the family of God. Our citizenship now is of heaven. Ephesians 2:18-19, declares, *"For through him we both have access by one Spirit unto the Father. Now therefore ye are no more strangers and foreigners, but FELLOW CITIZENS with the saints and the household of God."*

Satan and sin no longer have a right to control us any longer, we now belong to the Kingdom of God. There has come a change of ownership, a new creation man has become a son and daughter of God. He now has been granted right-standing with God. The fellowship that Adam and Eve lost in the garden, due to their disobedience, has been made available to all men by the precious blood of Jesus. Adam and Eve died spiritually when they ate of the tree of the knowledge of Good and evil. From that moment on, mankind has been born into sin without the possibility of escape. Sin nature was lodged in them; they were now sinners by nature, inheriting the nature of their new spiritual father, Satan.

But praise the Lord, God sent His only begotten Son, without sin and born of a virgin, to pay the full price for mans' sins. Jesus died, went to hell and on the third day was resurrected from the grave. Adam and Eve's fall from grace, could no longer have a hold on any man that would simply receive him as Lord and Savior. Jesus came to restore man to a right relationship with God and bring many sons and daughters unto glory. Romans 5:17-19, declares, *"For by one man's offence (Adam) death reigned by one; much more they which received abundance of grace and the gift of righteousness SHALL REIGN IN LIFE by one, Jesus Christ."* The New Century Translation declares, *"One man disobeyed God and many become sinners. In the same way one man, Jesus, obeyed and many were made right."*

What a plan—the redemption of mankind. What an honor to receive the free gift of right-standing with the Creator and to share His nature. All that is old has passed away, and now through Jesus we are new creatures.

FAMILY GENETICS AND INHERITANCE

On February 14, 2002, I witnessed the birth of my first baby daughter, Ashley Anna D'Amico. Ashley joined our family, weighing 6 pounds and 9 ounces. As I watched the miracle of the birth of my daughter, I got a greater glimpse of what our Heavenly Father must feel in His heart for His children. And just as we planned for Ashley's birth, God planned from the beginning of time for His own family. Just as our three daughters, Ashley, Aubrey, and Lexi have the genetics and resemblance of their parents, so do God's sons and daughters bear His genetics, nature and resemblance.

The new Creation man is God's master design of all creation, just as we who are new creations in Christ Jesus, also share in the benefits of joining the family of God. Let's take a closer look at some of the family benefits of the New Creation Man.

FORGIVENESS OF SINS

The new creation was God's display of love and was revealed in the cancellation of our sin debt. Our sins are not just covered, but cancelled as if the debt never existed. Isaiah 43:25, declares, *"I, even I, am He that blotteth out thy transgressions (sins) for mine own sake, and will not remember thy sins."* The New English Bible Translation declares, *"I alone, I am He who for his own sake WIPES OUT YOUR TRANSGRESSIONS, who will remember your sins NO MORE."* Not only did God wipe away our sins through Jesus, but we have also been changed from sinner to saint." Psalm 103:12, declares, *"As far as the east if from the west, so far hath he removed our transgressions from us."* The New English Bible declares, *"Far as the east if from west, so far has he put our offenses away from us."*

RIGHT STANDING WITH GOD

The new creation now means we have right standing with God. In 2 Corinthians 5:21 it declares, *"For he hath made him to be sin for us, who knew no sin; that we MIGHT BE MADE THE RIGHTEOUSNESS OF*

GOD IN HIM." The Streets Translation declares***, "The father took the son who never had any evil in him and laid the evil of the universe on Him that we might be made the RIGHTEOUSNESS OF GOD."*** We can now come into the presence of God without a sense of inferiority, guilt or shame, because we are made righteous by faith in Jesus Christ.

We now have access into God's presence and can now legally approach the throne of God boldly. Hebrews 4:16 from the Moffatt Translation declares, ***"So let us approach the throne of grace WITH CONFIDENCE ..."*** The Berkley Translation declares, "***Let us approach the throne of grace with MUCH ASSURANCE ..."*** The Basic American Standard Translation declares, ***"Then let us come near to the seat of grace WITHOUT FEAR."***

Jesus broke down the walls of sin standing between the Father and mankind, so we could approach our loving Heavenly Father without intimidation. The new creation man now inherits the legal position of sons and daughters. They are accepted into the presence of God and legally given the honor to walk with and before Him with favor. Ephesians 1:6, declares, ***"To the praise of the glory of his grace, wherein he hath MADE US ACCEPTED IN THE BELOVED. The Knox, declares, "... by whom he has taken us into HIS FAVOUR in the person of his beloved son."***

PARTAKERS OF THE *"ZOE"* LIFE OF GOD

In John 10:10, Jesus declared, ***"The thief cometh not, but for to steal, and to kill, and to destroy: I have come that THEY MAY HAVE LIFE, and that they may have it MORE ABUNDANTLY."*** The Greek Word for life, is *"ZOE,"* which literally means, the same life of God Himself. This life spoken of is the very substance of God's nature. In John 5:26, Jesus, declared, ***"For as the Father hath life (Zoe) In Himself; so hath he given to the Son to have life (Zoe) in Himself."***

When we receive Jesus Christ as our Lord, the very presence and substance of God Himself comes to dwell within us. 1 Corinthians 6:17, 19 declares, ***"He that is joined unto the Lord is one spirit."*** One translation reads, ***"The self-same spirit."*** We then find in verse 19 of the same chapter, ***"What? know ye not that your body is the temple of the***

Holy Ghost, WHICH IS IN YOU, WHICH YE HAVE OF GOD, and ye are not your own." It is this *"ZOE"* life of God that changes us from victims of sin to victors over sin. We conquer over spiritual death because of the Spirit of Life. God's very own nature has now come inside of us to unite us with heaven.

AUTHORITY OVER SATAN AND DEATH

Now that we are new creations in Christ, forgiven of sin and in right-standing with God, filled with His Spirit, Satan does not have any legal hold or control over us any longer. Jesus made it clear that those who bear His name, belong to Him, and also receive His delegated authority in the earth. In Luke 10:19, Jesus declared, *"Behold I give unto you power to tread upon serpents and scorpions, and OVER ALL THE POWER OF THE ENEMY; and nothing shall by any means hurt you."* We now take our place as master over the powers of the devil and all his evil cohorts through the name of Jesus. We have been elevated in Christ to a position of dominion. We are no longer slaves to sin and the powers of Satan. Now that the old man has passed away, we are to have no connection or entanglement with sin any longer. We now master through the master who lives within us. In 1 John 4:4, it declares, *"Ye are of God, little children, and have overcome them: because GREATER IS HE THAT IS IN YOU, than he that is in the world."*

Satan is called the God of this world, and we live in this world, but are no longer to be dominated by this world's system. We now take hold of the Word of God and exercise our authority over Sin And Satan. James 4:7, declares, *"Submit yourselves therefore to God. RESIST THE DEVIL, and he will flee from you."* We must not only see we have authority in Christ, but accept and use that authority.

The Barclay Translation adds more, *"So then, ACCEPT THE AUTHORITY OF GOD. Take a stand against the devil, and he will run from you."* F.F Bosworth, who wrote the book, *Christ The Healer*, made an interesting statement along these lines when he said, *"Any man or women can be a master over the devil overnight."* Once you find out what belongs to you, you must put it into action immediately, and it will work! The Message Bible declares, *"Yell a loud 'no' to the devil and watch him scamper."* Determine to take your authority in Christ and exercise who you are in Christ and tell the devil you have had enough in Jesus' name!

SONSHIP RESTORED

In Romans 8:15, the Apostle Paul defines the new place of sonship established for us in Christ Jesus. *"For we have not received the spirit of bondage again to fear; but ye have received the SPIRIT OF ADOPTION, whereby we cry, ABBA, FATHER."* Just as adopted children are placed into a new family with the benefits of that home, those in Christ Jesus are granted the inheritance of heaven through adoption. In Galatians 6:1, from the Amplified Bible, the Apostle Paul gives proper instruction how to restore a brother in Christ that has fallen into sin. I believe we get an understanding of God's attitude of heart in relating to our sonship, restored at the new birth. *"Brethren, If any person is overtaken in misconduct or sin of any sort, you who are spiritual [who are responsive to and controlled by the Spirit] should SET HIM RIGHT and RESTORE and REINSTATE HIM, without a sense of superiority and with ALL GENTLENESS, keeping an attentive eye on yourself, lest you should be tempted also."*

Adam and Eve's misconduct in the garden of Eden caused all mankind to plummet into spiritual death; yet, God sent His Son to restore us back into fellowship with Himself. We get insight of four basic steps toward sonship in Galatians 6:1, *"That God desires to do for all man."*

The first, *"Set Him Right.* God wants us to repent of serving ourselves, to serving Him.

Second, *"Restore."* God desires our relationship to be restored and made the proper provision in Jesus Christ.

Third, *"Reinstate."* God has now reinstated the new creation man back to his legal position of sonship.

Fourth, *"Gentleness."* The love of God is limitless toward mankind and can be reflected by His gentle heart to call us His adopted sons and daughters. In 1 John 3:2, Jesus declared, *"Beloved, now are ye the SONS OF GOD ..."* Sonship brings with it rights and privileges. Sonship means acceptance and provision. We can find our place of security, identity and belonging all in our relationship to God as His sons and daughters.

RESTORATION OF HEALTH

Jeremiah 30:17, declares, *"For I will RESTORE HEALTH UNTO THEE, and I will HEAL THEE of thy wounds, said the Lord."* What a beautiful promise from God. Webster's Dictionary defines *restore* as: *to bring back as to a good condition or original state of being.* God not only provided for the new creation man to be restored back to his originally intended condition in spirit, soul and also in body (1 Thessalonians 5:23), but we no longer have to be controlled and oppressed by physical sickness. In 1 Peter 2:24, it declares, *"Who own self bare our sins in His own body on the tree, that we, being dead to sin, should live unto righteousness: by whose stripes YE ARE HEALED."* The stripes of Jesus provided divine healing for all of God's children. As new creation man and women, we have been restored back to health! By faith in God's Word, we must declare ourselves the healed of the Lord.

PROVISION FROM OUR HEAVENLY FATHER

In 3 John 1:2, it declares, *"Beloved, I wish above all things that thou MAYEST PROSPER and be in health, even as thy soul prospereth."* The Weymouth Translation declares, *"Dear loved ones, I pray that you may in all prospects PROSPER AND KEEP WELL."* Any good natural father delights in taking care of his children. How much more does our Heavenly Father, perfect and loving in all His ways, delight in taking excellent care of us!

Psalm 23:1, declares, *"The lord is my shepherd, I shall not want."* When we are following after God's leadership, obeying and honoring this Word, then we will be in want for nothing! The wonderful promise to the new creation man and women is that God is a provider and will never forsake His children. Psalm 34:10, declares, *"The young lions do lack, and suffer hunger: but they that SEEK THE LORD SHALL NOT WANT OF (FOR) ANY GOOD THING."*

In order to tap into God's heavenly provision, it requires obedience in two main areas—tithes and offerings. Without going into a great depth, we are commanded to bring our *tithes* and *offerings* to God. In doing so, God opens up the window gates of heaven, Satan, the devourer is rebuked, and God pours out a blessing that we cannot contain. (Malachi 3:3-10). When we obey the Word of God and follow the Holy Spirit's leading in our sowing above the tithe, then the blessings will begin to flow.

An entire chapter or even a book could be written on this subject, like all the others listed; yet, we just want to touch on them to make you aware of the benefit purchased for the new creation man by Jesus. Our part is to seek Him, to honor Him, to obey Him as Father, and God will more than do His part of blessing and providing for us, His children.

THE LOVE OF GOD

As new creations in Christ, we have the divine nature of God abiding in us, which is Love. In 1 John 3:14, it declares, ***"We know that we have PASSED FROM DEATH UNTO LIFE, BECAUSE WE LOVE THE BRETHREN. He that loveth not his brother abideth in death."*** Then in 1 John 4:16, it declares***, "And we have known and believed the love that God has for us. God is love; and he that dwelleth in Love dwelleth in God, and God in him***."

God's very character and nature is love, and we are now recreated in His image. Romans 5:5, declares, ***"And His hope maketh not ashamed; because the LOVE OF GOD HAS BEEN SHED ABROAD IN OUR HEARTS by the Holy Ghost."*** The Moffatt Translation declares, ***"… Since God's love floods our hearts through the Holy Spirit which has been given to us."*** The unconditional love of God now floods our hearts through the new creation.

We must determine to walk in divine love and allow ourselves to be moved by Love to meet the needs of a broken world around us. The God of love now has found His residency in us and moves through our being to a lost and hurting world that is dying and going to hell.

Chapter 2

WALKING IN DIVINE LOVE

"A new commandment I give unto you, that ye LOVE ONE ANOTHER; as I HAVE LOVED YOU, that ye also love one another. By this all men shall know ye are my disciples, if ye have love one to another"
(John 13:34-35).

"And so I am giving a new commandment to you now– love each other just as much as I love you. Your STRONG LOVE FOR EACH OTHER will prove to the world that you are my disciples"
(John 13:34-35, The Living Bible).

" And WALK IN LOVE, as Christ also hath LOVED US, and hath given himself for us an offering and a sacrifice to God for a sweet smelling savour" (Ephesians 5:2).

"Take away love and the earth is a tomb."
—Robert Browning

"Increase my capacity for love and decrease my impulse to throw stones, actual or mental."
—George Appleton

"If they can see you love them, you can say anything to them."
—Richard Baxter

"The pain associated with emotional trials and worries can almost always be lessened by a little love."
—Chris Edmund

The greatest commandment Jesus gave to us was to love God and to love others. There are four Greek words that are translated "love" in the New

Testament. Each one has a different meaning. Love translated from the Greek word ***Agape,*** is the unconditional love of God. ***Phleo*** defines the love displayed between fellowmen. ***Storge*** is the love found between family members. And ***Eros*** is a natural, physical love that is expressed between a man and a woman united in marriage. We see these four types of love working daily in our culture.

Jesus declared that the greatest of these is agape, the God-kind of love. The God-kind of love is unconditional. It loves regardless of any circumstance and or situation. It serves as the binding force that keeps all of our other relationships united. Only the love of God keeps our friendships, families, and marriages strong.

THE LOVE OF GOD FLOODS OUR HEARTS

The day we receive Jesus Christ as our Lord and Savior something wonderful happens. The very nature and life of God comes to live within our hearts. Romans 5:5 declares, ***"And hope maketh not ashamed; because the LOVE OF GOD IS shed abroad IN OUR HEARTS by the Holy Ghost which is given unto us."*** The Moffatt Translation declares, ***"… God's love floods our hearts through the Holy Spirit which has been given unto us."***

When Jesus came into our hearts by the power of the Holy Spirit, we instantly received the capacity to love on the same level as God Himself. God is love. And Love Himself came to dwell in our hearts—to reach out and touch, change, and minister to the world around us.

But this supernatural love must mature. We must develop God's love by walking in it daily. Love is not a feeling, but a choice, a force, made available by God. In 1 John 4:7, it declares, ***"Beloved, let us love one another: FOR LOVE IS OF GOD; and everyone that LOVETH IS BORN OF GOD, AND KNOWETH GOD."*** Love declares to the world around us that we are truly born of God and know Him. In 1 John 3:14, it says, ***"We know that we have passed from death unto life, because we LOVE THE BRETHERN. He that loveth not his brother abideth in death."*** The Wade Translation declares, ***"We know we have passed out of a state of spiritual death into spiritual life, because we LOVE THE BRETHERN."***

THE GOD-KIND OF LOVE DEFINED

God's love is described in 1 Corinthians 13:4-8, *"Love endures long and is patient and kind; love never is envious nor boils over with jealously, is not boastful or vainglorious, does not display itself haughtily. It is not conceited (arrogant and inflated with pride); it is not rude (unmannerly) and does not act unbecomingly. Love (God's love in us) does not insist on its own rights or its own way, for it is not self-seeking; it is not touchy or fretful or resentful; it takes no account of the evil done to it (it pays no attention to a suffered wrong). It does not rejoice at injustice and unrighteousness, but rejoices when right and truth prevail. Love bears up under anything and everything that comes, is ever ready to believe the best of every person, its hopes are fadeless under all circumstances and it endures everything (without weakening). Love NEVER FAILS (never fades out or becomes obsolete or comes to an end)"* (The Amplified Bible).

These scriptures help us recognize the love of God. We see the character of God Himself, the character that is within each one of us as believers. As we yield to what is the love of God and resist what is not, we allow the Lord to develop and display Himself in us.

SIGNS OF THE LAST DAYS

Look around you. It doesn't take much to see that God's love is rare in this world. Jesus said this lack of love would be a sign of the end of the age and His second coming. *"And because iniquity shall abound, THE LOVE OF MANY SHALL WAX COLD"* (Matthew 24:12). The Message Bible clearly states, *"For many others, the overwhelming spread of evil will do them in—NOTHING LEFT OF THEIR LOVE BUT A MOUND OF ASHES."* And the New English Translation declares, *"...MEN'S LOVE FOR ONE ANOTHER SHALL WAX COLD."* With the overwhelming practice of sin crowding Jesus from their hearts, men and women can do nothing but fail in their ability to love.

This is where the Body of Christ will shine. We must be love reaching out to those desperately in need of being loved. Only the love of God will move us to the hurting world just like Jesus did. We see in Matthew

9:36, *"But when he saw the multitudes, HE WAS MOVED WITH COMPASSION ON THEM, because they fainted, and were scattered abroad, as sheep having no shepherd."* The Phillips Translation declares, *"He was deeply moved with compassion."* When the compassion of God pervades our hearts, it will compel us to those who are hurting around us.

MAKING LOVE OUR GREATEST QUEST

All of us should seek to make love our greatest aim and goal in life. We are challenged in 1 Corinthians 14:1 to *"Follow after charity;" "Keep on pursuing love"* (Williams Translation); *"Hotly pursue love"* (Modern English Translation); *"Make love your aim"* (Moffatt Translation); *"Make love your greatest quest"* (Becks Translation).

What is our quest in life? Webster's Dictionary says **quest** means to: **research, investigate, a pursuit or exploration**. There is no greater pursuit, nothing greater to explore or investigate than the love of God. Our journey in life must be to receive, understand and give away the love of God.

Without love as our driving force, everything else we do is vain. The Apostle Paul said, *"Though I speak with the tongues of men and of angels, and have not charity, I am become as sounding brass, or a tinkling cymbal. And though I have the gift of prophecy, and understand all mysteries, and all knowledge; and though I have all faith, so that I could remove mountains, and have not charity, I am nothing. And though I bestow all my goods to feed the poor, and though I give my body to be burned, and have not charity, it profiteth me nothing"* (1 Corinthians 13:1-3). We can do many things that seem noble, but apart from the love of God, it means nothing.

A DEEPER UNDERSTANDING OF LOVE

Many of us have been taught for years to walk in the love of God. But we cannot give what we do not receive. A true understanding of God's love is birthed out of an intimate relationship with Him. As the Lord continually touches and transforms our lives by His unconditional love, we are able to pour out on others what has been poured anew into us.

In 2 Thessalonians 3:5, we read, *"**And the Lord DIRECT YOUR HEARTS INTO THE LOVE OF GOD, and into the patient waiting for Christ.**"* The Message Bible describes it this way, *"**May the Master take you by the hand and lead you along the path of God's love and Christ's endurance.**"* The Living Bible declares, *"**May the Lord BRING YOU INTO AN EVER DEEPER UNDERSTANDING OF THE LOVE OF GOD and the patience that comes through Christ.**"*

GETTING ROOTED AND GROUNDED IN LOVE

As we come to know how great God's love is for us, it becomes our response to every situation in life. As we are rooted in His love, it will bear a lasting effect on others, too. In Ephesians 3:17-19 declares, *"**That Christ may dwell in your heart by faith; that ye, BEING ROOTED AND GROUNDED IN LOVE, may be able to comprehend with all the saints what is the breadth, and length, and depth, and height; and to KNOW THE LOVE OF CHRIST, which passeth knowledge, that ye might be filled with all the fulness of God.**"*

Determine right now to know the love of God and to walk in the love of God. When we are rooted and grounded in His great love, no person or situation can pull us out of that place. And we will experience life as it was meant to be—filled with all the fullness of God.

BLESSING THOSE WHO HURT YOU

Life can hurt. And in Matthew 5:44, Jesus tells us what to do when we are hurt by others, *"**But I say unto you, Love your enemies, BLESS THEM THAT CURSE YOU, do good to them that hate you, and pray for them which despitefully use you, and persecute you.**"*

If someone has worked ill toward your life, Jesus said to ***love them, bless them, do good to them and pray for them.*** That's what love would do. The Message Bible declares, *"**I'm telling you to love your enemies. Let them bring out the best in you, not the worst. When someone gives you a hard time, respond with the energies of prayer, for then you are working out of your true selves, your God-created selves. This is what God does.**"*

In Ephesians 4:31-32, the Apostle Paul declared, ***"Let all bitterness, and wrath, and anger, and clamour, and evil speaking, BE PUT AWAY FROM YOU, with all malice: And BE YE KIND one to another, TENDERHEARTED, FORGIVING ONE ANOTHER, even as God for Christ's sake hath forgiven you."*** Don't engage in conflict and respond in carnality. Put love's "best foot" forward. God's love never fails. And neither will you—if you walk in the love of God.

Chapter 3

SPIRITUAL HUNGER

"As the deer panteth after the water of the brooks, so panteth my soul after thee, o God. MY SOUL THIRSTETH FOR GOD, for the living God: When shall I come and appear before God?"
(Psalm 42:1-2).

"When the child of God ceases to hunger and thirst after God, Satan takes control."
—Smith Wigglesworth

"The secret of spiritual success is a hunger that persists. God was and is looking for hunger and thirsty people."
—Smith Wigglesworth

Physical hunger is a powerful force. Men work long hours to fill their belly. People do unthinkable things to still their hunger. Spiritual hunger is an even more powerful force. Jesus declared, **"Blessed are those who HUNGER AND THIRST FOR RIGHTEOUSNESS, FOR THEY SHALL BE FILLED"** (Matthew 5:6, NKJV). How could He promise such a blessing? Since creation, man had unsuccessfully sought out ways to be right with God. Nothing satisfied the hunger or quenched the thirst to know God.

Then Jesus announced that those who truly hunger and thirst after righteousness would finally be satisfied. He could promise this because He Himself would grant righteousness through the sacrifice He offered of His own blood and body on the cross. He paid for our sin and opened the door for a right and intimate relationship with God again. 1 Corinthians 1:9, declares, **"God is faithful, by whom ye were CALLED INTO the FELLOWSHIP of his son Jesus Christ our Lord."**

But even though the door was opened for all, Jesus qualified the statement with, *"those that hunger and thirst"* for right-standing will be filled. It is only our spiritual hunger that will drive us to partake of

His free, but costly, gift of righteousness. Psalm 107:9, declares, *"For he satisfieth the longing soul, and FILLETH THE HUNGRY SOUL WITH GOODNESS."*

A NEED FOR PASSION

Our passions will navigate us in life. If you look closely at your life, you will find it's moving in the direction of your strongest passion. If you think about golf all day long, more than likely you will live on the golf course, wear the latest golf fashion, and read the latest golf magazine for new tips to your game. That's okay if you're a professional golfer and your life is directly driven to maximize your game.

Personally, I don't have a problem with any individual who really enjoys golf as an outlet, when they are balanced with our priorities or God's assignment in life. We all must define from God what we are called to do in life and devote ourselves to maximizing that assignment.

Webster's dictionary defines **passion** as: *intense emotion, zeal, enthusiasm, ardent love.* What is it that God has put in your heart to achieve? What seems to ever be before you that just won't go away in your heart. It will not happen automatically. It will happen when we recognize our calling in life, submit it to God and work hard to serve and develop. Psalm 69:9, declares, *"Zeal for your house has eaten me up."* The Basic American Translation, declares, *"I am on fire with passion for your house."* The P.K. Harrison Translation declares, *"Enthusiasm for your house has devoured me."* Taylor's Translation is outstanding, *"My zeal for God and his work burns hot within me."*

PASSION CAN BE SEEN

I believe you can trace all great accomplishments in life to men and women with great passion. Proverbs 22:29, declares, *"Seest thou a man DILIGENT IN HIS BUSINESS? He shall stand before kings; he shall not stand before mean men."* The basic American Standard Translation declares, *"Have you seen a man WHO IS AN EXPERT HIS BUSINESS? He will take his place before kings; his place will not be among low persons."*

It is said that John Wesley traveled over 250,000 miles on horseback to preach the Gospel. He averaged 20 miles a day for 40 years. He preached over 40,000 sermons, wrote 400 books and knew 10 languages. That's passion! Every great achievement in life is a byproduct of passion, burning in the heart of an individual.

Many historians consider Abraham Lincoln to be one of the greatest American Presidents ever. His success story did not happen overnight, and it was not without adversity. Many attribute his success to perseverance, and rightfully so, but I attribute it to *PERSEVERANCE* and *PASSION*. Here's his story. *In 1831, he failed in business; 1832, was defeated for legislature; 1833, he failed in business for the second time; 1836, he suffered a nervous breakdown; in 1840, he was defeated for election; in 1843, he was defeated for congress; 1848, he was again defeated for congress; in 1855, he was defeated for the senate; in 1856, he was defeated for Vice President; in 1858, he was again defeated for the senate. THEN in 1860, he was elected the President of the United States of America.*

Over the span of 29 years, Lincoln failed successfully. What was his secret? The answer, although easier said than done, is simple, *"Passion to serve his country."* Lincoln once said, *"Having chosen our course without guile and with a pure heart, let us renew our trust in God and go forward without fear, with a manly spirit."* He also said, *"Always bear in mind that our own resolution to succeed is more important than any other thing."*

Walt Disney, one of the great visionaries of our time said, *"All our dreams can come true, if we have the courage to pursue them."*

Vince Lombardi, one of the greatest coaches in the history of the national football league once said, *"Winning is not everything, but making the effort to win is."* When we are willing to pay the price of obedience to God, working hard to reach our God assignments in life, we can succeed and serve many. Philippians 4:13, from the Twentieth Century Translation declares, *"Nothing is beyond my power in the strength of him who makes me strong."*

On May 6, 1954, a medical student from Oxford University named Rodger Banister changed history when he broke the four-minute mile barrier. Before May of 1954, the sports world thought that running a mile in less than four-minutes could not be done. Rodger Banister thought differently, and his passion drove him into the history books! In Mark 9:23, Jesus said, *"If thou canst believe, All things are possible to him that believeth."*

Dr. Lester Sumrall, in over 65 years of ministry, went around the world, starting out with $12.00 in his pocket. After spending more than 60 years ministering in over 119 nations of the world, spreading the gospel of Jesus Christ, he was compelled by God—knowing the urgency of the hour—did the work of many men. His leadership resume included: Pastor, Christian Center Cathedral of Praise in South Bend, Indiana; Chairman of the Board, LeSEA Broadcasting; Chairman of the Board, LeSEA, Inc.; Publisher of *World Harvest Magazine*; President of World Harvest Bible College; author of more than 110 books, teachings and study guides. He also produced films, records, cassette tapes, and hundreds of videotapes of his teachings. He built up a network of television stations, as well as short-wave radio broadcasts. At the age of 81, when most men are tempted to relax their schedules, he was running harder and faster. That's achievement—that's passion! Dr. Sumrall died Sunday morning April 28, 1996, leaving behind a legacy of integrity, faithfulness and obedience, touching millions of souls for the Lord Jesus Christ. His *passion for souls* drove him across the finish line to mark his generation with the power of God.

George Washington Carver once said, *"No individual has any right to come into the world and go out of it without leaving behind him distinct and legitimate reasons for having passed through it."* Bobby Bowden one of the greatest college football coaches ever once said, *"Don't go to your grave with a life unused."*

PUTTING GOD FIRST

Passion for God means putting God first in our lives. In Matthew 6:33, Jesus declared, *"But SEEK YE FIRST THE KINGDOM OF GOD, and his righteousness; and all these things shall be added unto you."* The Common Translation declares, *"Then set your hearts on the God movement and its kind of life and all things will come to you as a matter of course."* The Message Bible declares, *"Give your entire attention to what God is doing right now, and don't get worked up about what may or may not happen tomorrow."*

We must place seeking God and His will for our lives first and foremost, and then we will walk in God's divine order and blessing. Colossians 3:1-2, declares, *"If ye then be risen with Christ, SEEK THOSE THINGS WHICH ARE ABOVE, where Christ is sixtieth on the right hand of God. SET YOUR AFFECTIONS ON THINGS ABOVE, not on the things on the earth."* The Living Bible of verse two declares, *"Let heaven fill your thoughts, don't spend your time worrying about things down here."* God is looking to have first place in our lives, and when we seek to acknowledge him in all our ways, He will direct our lives. Proverbs 3:6, declares, *"IN ALL YOUR WAYS ACKNOWLEDGE HIM and he shall DIRECT THY PATH."*

GETTING THINGS IN ORDER

If God is not first place in our lives, there is need to make some changes. We need to reevaluate what God calls priorities and fashion our lives after them. It is when we place things in the *proper order* in our lives that life begins to make more sense and work. In 1 Corinthians 14:40, it declares**,** *"Let all things be done decently and IN ORDER."* The William's Translation declares, *"Everything must always be done in a proper and ORDERLY WAY."*

We can trace all problems in our lives to this very principle. In the chiropractic care, patients experiencing various back problems can associate it to a specific location in the back that is out of order. The common indicator that the back is out of order is ongoing pain. When chiropractic care is given, an adjustment is made, the back is realigned in order, then pain leaves.

This is very true of our lives, when we are having pain in any area; there is a need for adjustment. When we go to God's Word for the answer and adjust our thinking and actions, we really are setting that area back into proper order to work correctly. When our lives are ordered in God's ways, then we will step into the peace of God. Psalm 37:23, declares, *"The steps of a good man are ORDERed by the Lord: and thou delighteth in his ways."*

When we put God first and look to His Word to set our lives on the right path, then we will allow Godly order to work in our lives. All church problems, family, marriage, business, financial, etc., can be traced to some area that is not in order with God's Word. The Word of God is the vehicle that always cuts to the heart of issues and sets us on the course of peace and blessing. Hebrews 4:12, declares, *"For the word of God is quick and powerful, and sharper that any two-edged sword. Piercing even to the dividing of soul and spirit, and the joints and marrow, and is a discerner of the thoughts and intents of the heart."*

SALT OF THE EARTH

Our righteousness before God, through Jesus, makes us witnesses before men to His wonderful saving power and the reality of His Kingdom. Jesus said, *"Let me tell you why you are here. You're here to be salt seasoning that brings out the God flavors of this earth. If you lose your saltiness, how will the people taste godliness? You've lost your usefulness and will end up in the garbage"* (Matthew 5:13, MSG).

We are the "God flavors" of this earth, pointing mankind to the goodness of God. Our spiritual hunger must constantly be stirred up, our passion for God kept strong. We must never lose our "saltiness." In keeping Jesus our first love, we stay useful to His Kingdom.

Where is your hunger level? Are you satisfying yourself in Christ or pursuing other things? Let's take a look at a few areas that will help us stay hungry for God.

AVOID BEING LUKEWARM

There is a danger of becoming spiritually dull. Jesus warned the Laodicean Church in Revelation 3:15, *"I know you inside and out, and find little to my liking. You're not cold, you're not hot—far better to be either cold or hot! You're stale. You're stagnant. You make me want to vomit"* (MSG). **Stagnant** means: *inactive, lethargic, sluggish, lifeless or dormant* (Webster's dictionary). That same warning must be heard today. We must guard our hearts against any sluggishness, any lethargy, in our desire for Christ. Are we just going through the motions of religion, or are we cultivating a vital, living relationship with God?

Complacency not only hurts us but also hinders God's work through us. In the hour we live in, we must stay aggressive in our pursuit of the Lord. We must keep a constant temperature check on our hunger—cold, hot or lukewarm?

Jesus declared, *"These people draw near to Me with their mouth, and honor Me with their lips, but their heart is far from Me"* (Matthew 15:8, NKJV). The Message Bible states, *"These people make a big show of saying the right thing, but their heart isn't in it."* And the New English Bible Translation states they *"… pay me lip service."* God knows and God cares about the sincerity of our devotion. Let's not take it lightly.

STAY COMMITTED TO YOUR FIRST LOVE

Jesus won't settle for second place in our lives. Jesus won't even settle for a "tie" for first place. He demands and He deserves unequivocally the most exalted place in our hearts. Jesus addressed the Ephesian church about this very issue, *"But you walked away from your first love—why? What's going on with you anyway?"* (Revelation 2:4, MSG) Taylor's Translation states, *"Yet there's something wrong. You don't love me as at first."*

Although the church at Ephesus was still laboring for the Kingdom of God, they had lost their intimate dependence upon the Lord. We can get so busy "doing" for the Lord that we forget He wants us to "be" in Him. Don't let other pursuits diminish your pursuit of Jesus. We are reminded, *"If then you were raised with Christ, seek those things which are above, where Christ is, sitting at the right hand of God. Set your mind on things above, not on things on the earth"* (Colossians 3:1-2, NKJV).

Jesus promised, *"But SEEK FIRST THE KINGDOM OF GOD and His righteousness, and all these things shall be ADDED UNTO YOU"* (Matthew 6:33, NKJV). Let's keep our first love first. And then every other need of life will graciously come to us from His hand and every issue of life be settled under His leadership.

STIR YOURSELF UP TO GODLINESS

There is no achievement in life without discipline and determination. Don't live life looking for others to walk with God for you. You have to pursue God for yourself. God will meet you when you stir yourself up to walk with Him. He will counsel you and strengthen you.

We all have to be admonished to stir up what God has placed inside of us. The Apostle Paul exhorted young Timothy not to draw back in fear but**, "… _stir up_ the gift of God which is in you through the laying on of my hands"** (2 Timothy 1:6).

Stir means *to change your position in any manner, to impart movement, to rouse, excite or stimulate to activity* (Webster's dictionary). Paul charged Timothy to change his spiritual position. He challenged Timothy to banish fear and to stir up the Champion, Jesus, within him and get back to the high calling upon his life.

God has a good plan for you. Stir yourself up in your faith, your prayers, and remember His greatness is there to enable you to successfully walk in His will. Get up on the inside, refocus and fight! Drive fear, doubt and unbelief from your thinking.

In 2 Peter 3:1 we read, *"Beloved, I now write to you this second epistle (in both of which I _stir up_ your pure minds by way of reminder)"* (NKJV).

FEED ON THE WORD

What have you given your thoughts over to lately? Has it been the Word of God or the voice of modern opinion? Jesus declared, **"Man shall not live by bread alone, but BY EVERY WORD THAT PROCEEDS FROM THE MOUTH OF GOD"** (Matthew 4:4, NKJV). Is the Word of God what sustains you? Do you turn to the Word to satisfy you like you would turn to bread to satisfy your physical hunger?

We are commanded by God to give ourselves over to mediation and confession of His Word. If we fail to study the Word of God, we open ourselves up to deception. How can we know a lie if we do not know the truth? (John 8:32, John 8:44). The Word of God sheds light upon our path and counsels us in the right way. It re-fires and refines our passion for God. Psalm 119:105 states, *"Your word is a lamp to my feet and a light to my path."*

Apart from the Word, our spiritual hunger can be quickly misplaced and stolen away from God. In 2 Corinthians 5:7, it reminds us, *"For we guide our lives by faith, and not by what we see"* (TCNT). The psalmist cries out, *"Direct my steps by your word, and let no iniquity have dominion over me"* (Psalm 119:133, NKJV). We let the Word of God order our steps into God's realm of victory by giving it first place in our lives, by feeding upon it daily.

FAST AND PRAY

Although Jesus never specifically commanded us to fast, He signified it as an important component in our spiritual walk, *"But you, <u>when you fast</u>, anoint your head and wash your face, so that you do not appear to men to be fasting, but to your Father who is in the secret place; and your Father who sees in secret will reward you openly"* (Matthew 6:17-18).

What is the purpose of fasting? It is putting aside the flesh and its appetites in order to intensely pursue God. Nothing pulls good meaning Christians away from their love for God more than the flesh. Fasting should be a secret pursuit between the believer and God for the aim of sharpening spiritual hearing, receiving counsel and pressing into the secret place with God. (Psalm 91:1-2; 35:13; 1 Corinthians 7:5).

Fasting serves an excellent purpose of mortifying the flesh and exalting the higher nature of man, which is his spirit. (1 Peter 3:4; Romans 12:1-3). In times of fasting, we give ourselves over to heart communion with the Lord. We fine-tune our spiritual hearing. (Romans 8:14-16).

Galatians 5:24-25 declares, *"And those who are Christ's have crucified the flesh with its passions and desires. If we live in the Spirit, let us also walk in the Spirit."* Crucifying fleshly desires is a constant exercise in our walk with the Lord.

We must be determined to live out of our spirit, fellowship with the Holy Spirit through prayer, and walk in power of the Spirit. Ephesians 6:18 declares, *"Praying always with all prayer and supplication in the Spirit, being watchful to this end with all perseverance and supplication for all the saints"* (NKJV).

STAY FULL OF THE HOLY SPIRIT

We live in a day that is full of evil distractions. We cannot walk open to everything, but must live circumspectly and wisely. We are exhorted, *"Therefore do not be unwise, but understand what the will of the Lord is. And do not be drunk with wine, in which is dissipation; but BE FILLED WITH THE SPIRIT"* (Ephesians 6:17-18, NKJV). The Weymouth Translation states, *"... drink deeply of the Spirit."*

When we fill our time with feeding on the Word, praying in the Spirit, worshipping and fellowshipping with God from our hearts, we are *"drinking in"* the very life, the very substance, of God. The Lord wants us to be continually filled with His Spirit. It is not just a one-time experience, but a day-by-day, moment-by-moment abiding and rejoicing in Him. This is how we stay full. This is how we stay satisfied. Ephesians 3:19 declares, *"... to know the love of Christ which passes knowledge; that you may be filled with all the fullness of God"* (NKJV). As we seek the Lord, the revelation of His endless love for us is revealed to our hearts again and again. And as we truly know His love, we are flooded with His fullness.

Look at these translations: *"... and so at last you will be filled up with God Himself."* (Taylor's Translation) *"... that you may be filled (through all your being) unto all the fullness of God (may have the richest measure of the divine Presence, and become a body wholly FILLED AND FLOODED with God Himself)!"* (AMP).

Chapter 4

INTEGRITY—THE SURE FOUNDATION FOR SUCCESS

"I know also, my God, that thou TRIEST THE HEART, and HAST PLEASURE IN UPRIGHTNESS. As for me, in the uprightness of mine heart I have willingly offered all these things: and now have I seen with joy thy people, which are present here, to offer willingly unto thee"
(1 Chronicles 29:17).

"Knowing, my God how you EXAMINE OUR MOTIVES, and you DELIGHT IN INTEGRITY, with INTEGRITY OF MOTIVE I have willingly given all."
(1 Chronicles 29:17, New Jerusalem Translation)

"Therefore, judge me, O Lord; for I HAVE WALKED IN MY INTEGRITY; I have trusted also in the Lord; I SHALL NOT SLIDE"
(Psalm 26:1).

"Clear my name, O God. I've kept a clean shop"
(Psalm 26:1, The Message Bible).

"Integrity is doing the right thing, even when no one is watching."
—C.S. Lewis

God is delighted when His people walk in integrity. It's sad to say that in today's society integrity is a vanishing commodity. The world is intensely pursuing personal pleasure and shortcuts to success at the expense of a personal moral standard. From corporate America to the sports arena, politics and the church world, scandal has emerged. In every situation, it can all be traced back to a lack of individual integrity.

Integrity can be defined as: ***honest, moral soundness, uprightness of heart, genuine, open, straight in conduct and speech, freedom from fraud and deceit.*** (Webster's Dictionary) In 1 Peter 2:12 it instructs us, ***"Having your conversation honest among the Gentiles: that whereas they speak against you as evildoers, they may BY YOUR GOOD WORK, which THEY SHALL BEHOLD, glorify God in the day of visitation."*** The Revised Standard Version declares, ***"Maintain good conduct among the Gentiles ..."*** And the Weymouth Translation implores us to, ***"Live honorable lives ..."***

LET YOUR LIFE SHINE

George Washington, a founding father of this great nation, once said, ***"I hope I shall always possess firmness and virtue enough to maintain what I consider the most enviable of all titles, the character of an honest man."*** Pope Alexander once said, ***"An honest man is the noblest work of God."*** And one unknown author wrote, ***"When wealth is lost, nothing is lost, when health is lost, it can be regained, when character is lost, all is lost."*** Norman Vincent Peale said, ***"Think positive about yourself, keep your thoughts and actions clean and ask the God Who made you to keep remaking you."***

The standard of moral soundness must be lifted and maintained if we are to truly honor God in the earth with our lives. In Matthew 5:14-16, Jesus declared, ***"Ye are the light of the world. A city that is set on an hill cannot be hid. Neither do men light a candle, and put it under a bushel, but on a candlestick; and it giveth light unto all that are in the house. Let YOUR LIGHT SO SHINE BEFORE MEN, that they may SEE YOUR GOOD WORKS, and GLORIFY YOUR FATHER which is in heaven."*** For the world to see the message of victory in Christ Jesus they must see us living honorable lives before God and man.

In 1 Thessalonians 4:7 it declares**,** ***"But God hasn't invited us into a disorderly, unkempt life, but into something holy and beautiful on the inside and out"*** (MSG).

INTEGRITY IN LIFESTYLE

In 1 Peter 1:14-15, it declares, *"Don't lazily slip back into those old grooves of evil, doing just what you feel like doing. You didn't know any better then; you do now. As obedient children, let yourselves be pulled into a way of life shaped by God's life, a life ENERGIZED and ABLAZE WITH HOLINESS. God said, 'I am holy; you be holy'"* (MSG). We are not to slip back into evils of the past that once controlled our behavior. We are to live a disciplined lifestyle governed by God's Word and the Holy Spirit. Our thought life must be continually directed to the Word of God and controlled by the power of the Holy Spirit. Sloppy living is not the way of a disciple of Jesus Christ.

By feeding on the things of God, we will keep our minds renewed, our bodies under, and our spirit-man built up. Romans 12:1-2 declares, *"I beseech you therefore, brethren, by the mercies of God, THAT YE PRESENT YOUR BODIES A LIVING SACRIFICE, HOLY, acceptable unto God, which is YOUR REASONABLE SERVICE. And be NOT CONFORMED TO THIS WORLD: but be ye TRANSFORMED BY THE RENEWING OF YOUR MIND, that ye may prove what is that good, and acceptable, and perfect, will of God."* Presenting our bodies and continually renewing our minds with God's Word are major keys to maintaining a strong moral integrity.

David declared, *"Wherewithal shall a young man cleanse his way? by taking heed thereto ACCORDING TO THY WORD. With my whole heart have I sought thee: O let me not wander from thy commandments. Thy WORD HAVE I HID IN MINE HEART, that I MIGHT NOT SIN AGAINST THEE"* (Psalm 119:9-11). One of the secrets of Smith Wigglesworth's walk in the power of God was his unbroken fellowship with God. His continual heart-felt devotion to God kept him not only in the place of power, but shaped his godly, sound character.

INTEGRITY IN SPEECH

We should be sound, complete and whole in speech. When we give a promise, we ought to follow through. Our integrity is only as good as our ability to keep our word. How many times have we seen this scenario: Someone gives his word to do one thing and ends up doing another? We should reflect the person found in Psalm 15:4. *"In whose eyes a vile person is contemned; but he honoureth them that fear the LORD. HE THAT SWEARETH TO HIS OWN HURT, AND CHANGETH NOT."* The P.K. Harrison Translation declares, *"One who will KEEP HIS PROMISE, even to his own detriment, and WILL NOT RETRACT."* We must be true to the pledge of our words, even if we suffer in keeping it.

In Titus 2:8, the Norlie Translation declares, *"Your message should be true, YOUR LANGUAGE CORRECT and not open to criticism."* What makes God a good God is his ability to give His Word and keep it in our lives. Our words and actions should line up with truth. Let's speak the truth, live the truth and honor God with sound speech that cannot be condemned. Stay clear of gossip, slander or any secret talk that spreads conflict of any kind. (Numbers 11:1, Leviticus 19:16, Proverbs 6:19, Proverbs 26:20, Proverbs 17:9).

In 1 Peter 3:10 it declares, *"FOR HE THAT WILL LOVE LIFE, AND SEE GOOD DAYS, LET HIM REFRAIN HIS TONGUE FROM EVIL, AND HIS LIPS THAT THEY SPEAK NO GUILE."*

INTEGRITY IN FINANCES

The Word of God is filled with instruction on integrity in financial management. Of the 38 parables Jesus taught, 16 of them have to do with money. In the New Testament, more is said about money than the topic of Heaven or Hell. Five times more is said about money than prayer. There are 500 verses on both prayer and faith and over 2,000 verses deal with money. Get the picture? It doesn't mean that those other topics are not important, but God knows man has a greater struggle with handling money.

The way we handle our finances is directly related to our love for God. God doesn't have a problem with His believers having money—He just doesn't want money to have them. Jesus told us, *"For where your treasure is, there will your heart be also"* (Matthew 6:21). The Philips Translation declares, *"For wherever your treasure is, you may be certain that your hearts will be there too!"* We must not let the love of money and its ability to bring comforts of life steal our heartfelt simple devotion to God. Money in itself is not evil, but the inordinate lust for it or obtaining it by questionable means is. In 1 Timothy 6:10 it clarifies, ***"For the LOVE OF MONEY is the root of all evil: which while some COVETED AFTER, they have ERRORED from the faith, and pierced themselves through with many sorrows."***

God made us to be stewards over the money He has provided for us—not owners. We must act nobly and honorable in our handling of it. Psalm 24:1 declares, ***"The earth is the Lord's, and the fullness thereof; the world, and they that dwell therein."*** If we fail to remember this, we will get sidetracked and miss God. What does it profit a man if he gains the whole world and yet loses his soul? In 1 Timothy 6:7 it reminds us, ***"For you have brought nothing into this world, and it is certain we can carry nothing out."***

The rich, young ruler walked away from following Jesus. Jesus asked him to give all his wealth away and to come and follow Him. (Matthew 5:17-23). Little did the rich, young ruler know that God was setting him up for and even greater harvest. (Luke 6:38). Jesus was addressing the one issue in his life that would keep him from becoming a disciple. The problem was not the money itself, but that he trusted in his riches more than God. If he had put God first place in his life, he would have had both God and wealth. This man walked away from the call of God because he had great possessions.

Jesus said Satan would use the deceitfulness of riches to choke the Word's fruitfulness in our lives. ***"And these are they which are sown among thorns; such as hear the word, And the cares of this world, and the deceitfulness of riches, and the lusts of other things entering in, choke the word, and it becometh unfruitful"*** (Mark 4:18-19). The E.V. Rieu Translation calls it, ***"… the lure of riches."*** The New English Bible describes it as, ***"… the false glamour of wealth."***

The heart of the rich young ruler was thorny ground. He walked away from Jesus, the Living Word, preferring to serve his wealth over God. With so much emphasis being placed on prosperity, we must be careful that we do not get out of balance. We are called to seek God's face, not wealth. God desires to bless His saints. (Psalm 35:37). But it is a blessing of purpose, a blessing that spills over to others. Deuteronomy 8:18 declares, *"But thou shalt remember the LORD thy God: for it is he that giveth thee power to get wealth, that he may establish his covenant which he sware unto thy fathers, as it is this day."*

We are called to be honorable stewards of all God blesses us with. Our wealth is to further the work of the Kingdom of God to establish His covenant in the earth. We must never forget it is about stewardship—not ownership. It is about covenant, not covetous.

INTEGRITY IN THE WORKPLACE

Work ethics have declined drastically in today's culture. People are going to work with one goal in mind … to get the paycheck for doing as little as possible. Loyalty and a conviction to work above and beyond the call of duty is virtually non-existent. Abraham Lincoln once said, *"My father taught me to work hard; he didn't teach me that I would always love it."* Zig Ziglar once said, *"When we do more than we are paid to do, eventually we will be paid more for what we do."* Frank Lloyd Wright said, *"A professional is one who does his best work when he feels the least like working."*

How many times have you stood in a checkout line and asked the cashier, "How are you doing today?" And their response goes something like this … "I'll be better in 20 minutes when I get off of this job!" The attitude of today is, "I am working for you to do you a favor. Don't ask me to do more than is expected. I can't wait to get out of here." As Christians, we ought to display the greatest worth ethic on the planet. Colossians 3:22-23 declares, *"Servants, obey in all things your masters according to the flesh; NOT WITH EYE SERVICE, as men pleasers; but in singleness of heart, fearing God; And whatsoever ye do, do it heartily, as to the Lord, and not unto men."* The Message Bible admonishes us to, *"Servants, do what you're told by your earthly masters. And don't just do the minimum that will get you by. DO YOUR BEST. WORK FROM THE HEART for your REAL MASTER, for GOD, confident that you'll get paid in full when you come into your inheritance."*

We must always keep in mind that we are really working for God and not man. He is watching the faithfulness and unfaithfulness of men.

Proverbs 22:13 warns us, ***"The lazy man is full of excuses. 'I can't go to work!' he says. 'If I go outside, I might meet a lion in the street and be killed!'"*** (TLV). Hard work means putting away a lazy attitude and getting busy.

Proverbs 12:24 declares, ***"Work hard and become a leader, be lazy and never succeed."*** All successful individuals have committed themselves to an honest day's work. They are not clock watchers but pacesetters. Proverbs 14:23 declares, ***"In all our labour there is profit, but the talk of the lips tendeth to poverty."*** The Message Bible states, ***"Hard work pays off, mere talk puts no bread on the table."***

INTEGRITY IN OUR RELATIONSHIPS

When integrity rules our relationships, we will not take advantage of other people. We will not seek our own benefit, but what is to their benefit. When we walk in the love of God, we seek to be a blessing and add value to others. In 2 Corinthians 7:2 declares, ***"In no instance have we wronged or harmed or TAKEN ADVANTAGE OF ANYONE"*** (The Twentieth Century Translation). There are basically two types of people in the world—givers and takers. Remember, no one owes us anything in life. Our confidence and complete trust must be in God alone.

When we look to God and trust in Him in all of our relationships, we will be a blessing to all those around us. The love of God doesn't allow us to use anyone for our own gain, but causes us to give to the benefit of others. We should not seek others out for what they can do for us, but seek them out for what we can do for them.

In 2 Corinthians 12:14, the Apostle Paul said, ***"Now I am all ready to visit you for the third time, and I am still not going to be a burden to you. It is you I WANT—not your money"*** (J.B. Phillips Translation).

The Holy Spirit will join us to those whom He desires if we will let Him. True success comes when we have found "our company" and walk with those contending for the same cause. I heard it said, ***"Success in life is simply found in a series of great relationships."*** Another unknown author said, ***"Relationships are like an elevator. They will take you up or they will take you down."*** We will be a constant refreshing to those around us as we walk with God.

The Apostle Paul knew the power of a relationship built on integrity. ***"I am GLAD OF THE COMING of Stephanas and Fortunatus and Achaicus: for that which was lacking on your part they have supplied. FOR THEY HAVE REFRESHED MY SPIRIT and YOURS: therefore, acknowledge ye them that are such"*** (1 Corinthians 16:17-18). The three men filled the needs of the saints at Corinth and refreshed Paul. They came to serve and be a blessing to the church and the man of God. These men were not consumed with their own needs.

Katherine Kuhlman once said, ***"The only great possession I have in this life is my intense love for people."*** Integrity in our relationships shows itself in our sincerity, loyalty, and trueness of heart towards others. It makes us givers and a blessing in every way.

INTEGRITY IN MOTIVE

Proper motives are so very important in life. Our motives can be revealed in *"why we do the things we do."* Webster's dictionary defines ***motive*** as: ***a consideration which determines choice or induces action.*** Proverbs 16:2 points out how easily we can deceive ourselves, ***"A man's conduct may strike him as pure, Yahweh, however, WEIGHS THE MOTIVES"*** (Jerusalem Translation). God always looks past the outward conduct to the inward motivation of the heart.

It is good to evaluate our motives and remind ourselves of God's desires constantly. The United States Military Academy at West Point placed their motivation for training in three words: ***"Duty, Honor, Country."***

We ought to ask ourselves, ***"What is God calling me to do in life for Him? How can I carry out this assignment with the most honorable of motivations? How can I make the world around me a better place? Am I motivated by God's goodness to help others?"***

Jesus' highest motivations was the redemption of all mankind. He was selfless and pure. Philippians 2:3-5 reminds us, ***"Let nothing be done through strife or vainglory; but in lowliness of mind let each esteem other better than themselves. Look not every man on his own things, but every man also on the things of others. Let this mind be in you, which was also in Christ Jesus."*** The Message Bible states it this way,

"Don't push your way to the front; don't sweet-talk your way to the top. Put yourself aside, and help others get ahead. Don't be obsessed with getting your own advantage. Forget yourselves long enough to lend a helping hand." That's God's way!

The Apostle Paul chose to send Timothy to the Philippian Church because he knew Timothy to be a man of integrity. Paul recognized Timothy's pure motivation. He wasn't wrapped up in self-interest, but rather an intense interest in the welfare of the Body of Christ. Philippians 2:20-21 from the Message Bible states, *"I plan (according to Jesus' plan) to send Timothy to you very soon so he can bring back all the news of you he can gather. Oh, how that will do my heart good! I HAVE NO ONE QUITE LIKE TIMOTHY. He is LOYAL, and GENUINELY CONCERNED FOR YOU. Most people around here are LOOKING OUT FOR THEMSELVES, with little concern for the things of Jesus."*

Timothy was pure in his quest to look after the welfare of others. Paul knew Timothy's tested worth and proven motives. He was there simply to help Paul advance the Gospel. Ecclesiastes 12:13 declares, *"Let us hear the conclusion of the whole matter: FEAR GOD, and KEEP HIS COMMANDMENTS: for this is the whole duty of man."*

Chapter 5

FAITHFULNESS—GOD'S PROVING GROUND FOR PROMOTION

"And I thank Christ Jesus our Lord, who hath enabled me, for that he COUNTED ME FAITHFUL, putting me into the ministry"
(2 Timothy 1:12).

"For PROMOTION COMETH neither from the east, nor from the west, nor from the south. But God is judge: he putteth down one, and setteth up another"
(Psalm 75:6-7).

"I know of nothing which I choose to have as a subject of my ambition for life than to keep faithful to my God till death."
—C.H. Spurgeon

"God rewards faithfulness not the size of our ministries."
—Daniel Affi

"Great Faith is a product of great fights."
—Smith Wigglesworth

Without question, one of the foremost qualifications for promotion is faithfulness. It is not only a requirement with God, but also the strength of character that leads to fulfillment and much blessing in our lives. Proverbs 28:20 declares, *"A FAITHFUL MAN shall abound with blessing."* Yet, today, we have seen an alarming erosion of faithfulness in our culture and society. In the workplace, disloyalty works daily, undermining company morale and profits. *"Just present me with my paycheck, and I'll be happy. And please don't ask me to have to really work today."*

Over 60 percent of our marriages are ending in divorce due to unfaithfulness, or just an unwillingness to remain committed. The business world is plagued with corporate scandal and lust for power, and the list goes on! What seems to be the problem? Jesus makes the answer clear in Mark 9:19, *"O FAITHLESS GENERATION."* When culture steps away from faithfulness to God's Word and embraces the way of least resistance, we are headed for trouble. In order to experience success in life, whether it pertains to business, marriage, family, working in ministry or the local church, or any other area of life, we must be faithful. We must lift the standard and embrace faithfulness to God and His principals in every area of our lives.

Webster's dictionary defines ***faithfulness*** as: ***true to affections or allegiance; trustworthy; loyal; steadfastness; reliable or firm to an adherence or promise***. Let's determine to give our best to God. Whatever He has assigned for you in life, seek to be faithful no matter the cost. God will receive much glory through your obedience, and you will continue to grow and mature. Decide you will be found of God proven faithful even in the little things, so He can entrust you with more. The following are some foundational truths to consider concerning the subject of faithfulness.

FAITHFULNESS CATCHES GOD'S ATTENTION

Faithfulness catches God's attention and welcomes us into His presence. Psalm 101:6 declares, *"MY EYES SHALL BE UPON THE FAITHFUL OF THE LAND, that they may dwell with me."* The Berkley Translation declares, *"I will look to the trustworthy of the land to be my associates."* The Living Bible declares, *"I will make the godly of the land my heroes and invite them to my house."* Faithfulness gets God's attention. Those who are proven faithful are the individuals that God invites into His presence and deems His associates in the earth.

It is upon the faithful that God will place His presence to use in these last days! He concentrates His attention on those who have His heart and are proven trustworthy, calling them his allies, heroes and associates. He will never lose sight of His love for all mankind, whether Christian or not, yet His focus will fall upon those who will honor Him faithfully. It is to those He entrusts His business to manage down in the earth. We must be faithful in the hour of unfaithfulness, and diligently work unto the Lord. It has been said that more people fail in life for a lack of faithfulness—not for a lack of ability.

FAITHFULNESS MEANS RESPONSIBILITY

Faithfulness is a biblical key to fulfilling all that God has assigned for us. It is the proper foundation upon which God lays responsibilities in our lives. Promotion from God only means responsibility at a new level. It is not to be confused with the world's definition of exalting oneself. In Jeremiah 45:5 the scripture is clear, *"And seekest thou great things for thyself? Seek them not."* Then in Luke 14:11 Jesus declares, *"For whosoever exalteth himself shall be abased; and he that humbleth himself shall be exalted."*

It is stewardship with God and not self-promotion. God is looking for us to be *faithful and responsible, trustworthy over His affairs.* God is not interested in endorsing our agendas—only His will. When we prove ourselves responsible, we qualify for more delegated authority. This is achieved when we apply godly wisdom in our lives. Wisdom from God's Word will bring true honor from the Lord. Proverbs 4:7-8 declares, *"WISDOM is the principal thing; therefore, GET WISDOM: and with all thy getting get understanding. Exalt her, and she shall PROMOTE THEE: she shall bring thee HONOUR, when thou dost embrace her."*

In Luke 9:23 Jesus declared, *"And he said to them all, 'If any man will come after me, let him deny himself, and take up his cross daily, and follow me.'"* The Message Bible declares, *"Anyone who intends to come with me has to LET ME LEAD. You're not in the driver's seat, I AM."* The Bible is very clear that God will use us only as we consecrate ourselves to do His will. He is actively searching for those He can trust to carry out His orders in a loyal, true attitude of a servant's heart. God is looking to advance His Kingdom with the wisdom from above, not from men!

FOCUS ON CHARACTER DEVELOPMENT OVER GIFTING

We can never hear enough on the subject of character development. Character development is not an overnight achievement, but an achievable pursuit with God. The right foundation for all that we are and do must come from a strong character. In 1 Corinthians 12:27 it declares, *"Now ye are the body of Christ, and members in particular."* All of us have a function in the body and specific gifts from God. But a common mistake is to place greater emphasis on our gifting rather than on developing our character.

Webster's dictionary defines **character** as**:** ***good behavior, honesty, good reputation, and moral strength.*** There are many precious believers who possess wonderful gifts from God, holding great promise; yet, they fall short of being used by God. They are more interested in their ability to be recognized than submitting their gifts in humility to God.

One potential problem is *finding our identity or self-worth* from our giftings, instead of *who we are in Christ*. If we think our giftings define who we are, we will *push for approval,* instead of learning to *develop in character,* renewing our minds in Christ Jesus. We must always remember **giftings are what we can do, character is who we are.** When we are faithful to serve, prioritizing our character over our abilities, we position ourselves to be used by God.

God is far more interested in our inward life than our gifting anyway. Ultimately, our gifts make room for us when we have the right heart. Character development is always the right foundation for service to God. Proverbs 4:23 declares, ***"Keep thy heart with all diligence; for out of it are the issues of life."*** The Amplified Bible declares, ***"KEEP and GUARD YOUR HEARTS with all vigilance and above all that you guard, for out of it flows the springs of life."*** The Message Bible declares, ***"Keep vigilant watch over your heart; that's where life starts."***

If we fail to prove ourselves trustworthy in character, it is sure, no matter how strong our gifts, God will put us on hold. He is protecting His interests as well as our well-being. Abraham Lincoln once said, ***"Nearly all men can stand adversity, but if you want to test a man's character give him power."*** Position and power ultimately mean influence. A lot of serious responsibility surrounds the privilege of using our giftings and abilities. God will not promote us until we prove ourselves faithful. God promotes our faithfulness before He promotes our giftings. It is a grave mistake to promote gifted individuals before investigating the fruit of faithful service in their lives. It sets them up for destruction.

The Apostle Paul writing to Timothy made an interesting statement concerning the qualifications of the deacons in the church. *"And let them also FIRST BE PROVED; then let them use the office of a deacon, being FOUND BLAMELESS"* (1 Timothy 3:10). The Message Bible states, *"They must be reverent before the mystery of the faith, NOT USING THEIR POSITION TO TRY TO RUN THINGS. Let them PROVE THEMSELVES FIRST."* Most problems arise when subordinates use their position of influence to *try to run the show instead of serving*.

This scenario is common in the local church and a source of constant frustration among its leaders. It has been said, *"Behind all called and able leaders, there are called and able leaders."* With that in mind, we must recognize the importance of submitting our gifts to those in authority over us. We need to **settle down and serve.** We may only be required by God to support an institution for a certain season, but we must *"bloom where we are planted"* and *be faithful*. God will bless that organization and us mightily.

Thank God it's never too late to learn these principals. Ecclesiastes 3:1 declares, *"To every thing there is a season, and a time to every purpose under the heavens."* Remember, every season of serving others is for *seasoning and growth* in our lives. We must **know our place**. Work hard unto the Lord. And honor those who we are serving. If we will just be faithful and help others obey God, God will bless us.

Remember gifts are given to exalt Jesus Christ—not any man or woman. In 2 Corinthians 4:2 from the Amplified Bible it declares, *"Moreover, it is essentially required of stewards that a man should be found faithful proving himself worthy of trust."* It is the novice that will fall into the trap of self-promotion, instead of heaven's promotion. Serving God in supportive roles requires maturity and loyalty. When we embrace these assignments with a teachable heart, we will learn the seriousness of leadership by **sympathizing** rather than **criticizing**. John Ruskin said, *"The highest reward for a man's toil is not what he gets from it, but what he becomes."*

RECOGNIZE STEWARDSHIP OVER OWNERSHIP

When we recognize that all we are and all the good we receive is from God, we realize that we are simply stewards, not owners. James 1:17 declares, *"Every good gift and every perfect gift is from above, and cometh down from the Father of lights, with whom is no variableness, neither shadow of turning."* We must readjust our thinking from owner to manager. We should not be like the unreliable servant who buried his talent, instead of using it for God. Submit it to God and serve.

Colossians 3:22-23 declares, *"And whatsoever ye do, do it heartily, AS TO THE LORD, and not unto men; knowing that OF THE LORD ye shall receive THE REWARD of the inheritance: for ye serve the Lord Christ."* The Message Bible states in verse 23, *"Do your best work from the heart for your real Master, for God, confident that you'll get paid in full when you come into your inheritance."*

In all of our endeavors we must act as stewards over God's business, not owners over our own. We need to take serious what God has given us and be *good managers* with it all. We must do it wholeheartedly unto God and not as unto men. Let's be good stewards of the manifold wisdom of God, always being faithful.

In 1 Timothy 6:7, it declares, *"For we brought nothing into this world, and it is certain we can carry nothing out."* Only the fruit of our lives will remain.

SERVE IN ANOTHER MAN'S FIELD

Until we sow our service into another man's field, we do not qualify for our own from God. There have been those who are faithful, but in many cases, only to promote themselves. Thomas Jefferson once said, *"The selfish spirit of commerce knows no country and feels no passion or principle but gain for self."* Serving under another man's calling or vision can provide us the greatest lessons in life. True maturity is developed out of our obedience and commitment to submit ourselves under a greater authority. Hebrews 13:17 declares, *"OBEY THEM THAT HAVE THE RULE OVER YOU, SUBMITTING YOURSELVES: for they watch over your soul, as they must give account, that they may do it with joy, and not with grief: for that is unprofitable for you."* There are no shortcuts in God's methods. We either faithfully spend seasons serving in another man's field or we will never be entrusted with our own.

Jesus declares, **"And if you have not PROVEN FAITHFUL in that which belongs to another, who will give you that which is your own?"** (Luke 16:12, AMP). We must never look to take advantage of those we serve or advance ourselves, but to sincerely help others obey the Lord. Jeremiah 45:5 declares, **"… Should you then seek great things for yourself? … Do not seek them!"** (NIV). We must never act out of selfish means. We must never seek to use another man's many years of labor as a platform to promote ourselves. There is a great reward for those willing to genuinely give themselves faithfully to serve in another man's assignment from God.

Albert Einstein once said, **"Only a life lived for others is a life worth living."** The true heart of a servant will embrace this principle. We will take even undesirable tasks and do them with a good attitude to promote the progress of the one we are serving. If we're not willing to work hard, sacrificing our own comforts in another man's field, then we are still not ready for promotion from God.

Matthew 23:11 declares, **"BUT HE THAT IS GREATEST AMONG YOU SHALL BE YOUR SERVANT."** Webster's dictionary defines s*ervant* as: **to satisfy the needs of others; to render service so as to benefit, help, or promote the course of others; to exert oneself continually.** The Message Bible states in Matthew 23:11, **"DO YOU WANT TO BE A STANDOUT? THEN STEP DOWN AND BE A SERVANT."** We must serve faithfully those whom God has placed over us and give them our best.

MAINTAIN A HUMBLE ATTITUDE OF HEART

"By HUMILITY AND the FEAR OF THE LORD are riches, and honor, and life" (Proverbs 22:4).

"Let this mind be in you, which was also in Christ Jesus: who, being in the form of God, thought it not robbery to be equal with God: but MADE HIMSELF OF NO REPUTATION, and took upon him the FORM OF A SERVANT, and was made in the likeness of men" (Philippians 2:5-7).

Humility before the Lord is an indicator of a truly faithful individual. Proverbs 25:6-7 declares, ***"Put not thyself in the presence of the king, and stand not in the place of great men: for better it is that it be said unto thee, 'Come up hither; than that thou shouldest be put lower in the presence of the prince whom thine eyes have seen.'"***

God never wants us to push ourselves forward, driven by self-assertiveness or boastful ambition, but to walk softly and humbly before God and man. Jesus declared in Luke 14:11, ***"If you walk around with your nose in the air, you're going to end up flat on your face"*** (MSG). Proverbs 29:23 declares, ***"A MAN'S PRIDE SHALL BRING HIM LOW: BUT HONOR SHALL UPHOLD THE HUMBLE OF SPIRIT."***

Walking in humility is always a matter of personal choice. We will either point others to the greatness of God or to ourselves, which ultimately leads to our destruction. Proverbs 18:12 states, ***"BEFORE DESTRUCTION THE HEART OF MAN IS HAUGHTY, AND BEFORE HONOR IS HUMILITY."*** We must always draw all attention to Jesus and give Him the entire honor and praise which is truly due to His name. We are instructed from the Word of God to humble ourselves and be clothed with humility. Humility is the garment worn by the faithful servants of the Lord!

1 Peter 5:5-6 declares, ***"Likewise, ye younger, submit yourselves unto the elder. Yea, all of you be subject one to another, and be CLOTHED WITH HUMILTY; for God resisteth the proud and giveth grace to the humble. HUMBLE YOURSELVES therefore under the mighty hand of God, that he may exalt you in due time."***

BE RELIABLE

No matter how blessed we are with abilities from heaven, if we can't be reliable, then our usefulness in the Kingdom of God will be ineffective. Proverbs 25:19, from the Living Bible Translation declares, ***"Putting confidence in an unreliable man is like chewing with a sore tooth or trying to run on a broken foot."*** The King James Version declares, ***"Confidence in an unfaithful man in time of trouble is like a broken tooth and a foot out of joint."*** If we prove to be unreliable in any organization or relationship, we bring pain instead of blessing.

Webster's dictionary defines ***reliable*** as: ***suitable or fit to be relied upon; dependable; trustworthy.***

It is in the time of trouble or challenge that faithfulness is needed the most. It is in those times that our true character, our reliability, is revealed. Our gifting is irrelevant if we cannot be counted on when we are needed the most.

The Apostle Paul endured much affliction in his life and ministry. Many men left his side, just as they left the side of Jesus in the Garden of Gethsemane. The Apostle Paul declared, ***"At first answer no man stood with me, but ALL FORSAKE ME: I pray God that it may not be laid to their charge"*** (2 Timothy 4:16). We see Luke emerge as the reliable one for the Apostle Paul in difficult times, ***" … for Demas, because he loved this world, HAS DESERTED ME and has gone to Thessalonica. Crescens has gone to Galatia, and Titus to Dalmatia. Only Luke is with me"*** (2 Timothy 4:10-11, NIV).

Let's be faithful to our commitments. Let's give God our best by proving our reliability. If we say we are going to do something, then let's do it quickly and proficiently. We bring honor to the Lord by our proven faithfulness to Him. Psalm 15:4b declares, ***"He that sweareth to his own hurt, and changeth not."*** Our words hold no weight when they are not backed with action.

HAVE A PROPER ATTITUDE

John Maxwell made an interesting statement on attitude, ***"Attitude is the speaker of our present: it is the prophet of our future."*** Our attitude will always determine the progress we make in life for the Lord. It will make or break our lives. Lou Holtz, the former head football coach for Notre Dame said, ***"Ability is what you're capable of doing, motivation determines what you do and attitude determines how well you do it."*** A faithful servant will maintain the proper attitude in his commitments in life. He will show proper respect for God, His Word, His work and all those he has placed in authority over them.

Webster's dictionary defines ***attitude*** as: ***one's disposition; bodily posture; mental posture; and a way of thinking.*** Philippians 2:5 declares, ***"Let this attitude be in you which was also in Christ."*** The Living Bible declares, ***"Your attitude should be the kind that was shown us by Jesus Christ."*** Jesus was the epitome of faithfulness to His Father. His attitude was to fulfill the mandate of His Heavenly Father and die on the cross to save all humanity from their sins. Philippians 2:8-9 declares, ***"And being found in the fashion as a man, he humbled himself, and BECAME OBEDIENT unto death, even the death of the cross. Therefore, God highly exalted him, and given him a name above all names."***

It was the joy set before Him that He endured the cross with a humble, obedient heart unto God. Out of His submissive attitude of heart and obedience to the great plan of redemption, we now enjoy the eternal fruits of righteousness! Stay positive, teachable, enthusiastic, looking for the best to come your way. Remember, it isn't always what we are saying or doing that is wrong, but the demeanor in which it is projected. Maintaining a good attitude is a personal key to success and fulfillment. Be a green light person, and you will be used by those obeying God.

PUT AWAY SELFISHNESS

Thinking like a child means an individual is constantly concerned about themselves and about their needs being fulfilled. When they become self-centered and selfish, they can become high maintenance for those around them. We should adopt the motto and attitude, ***"I am a low maintenance, and high output Christian."*** When we grow into maturity, we lose sight of ourselves and look always to helping others obey God in life. In 1 Corinthians 13:11, the great chapter known for *the love of God,* it declares, ***"When I was a child, I spake as a child: but when I became a man, I put away childish things."*** The Weymouth Translation declares, ***"… I talked like a child, felt like a child, reasoned like a child."*** The Johnson Translation declares, ***"For instance, when I was a child, it was quite proper for me to think and act like a child; but when I became adult, I stopped functioning like a child."***

After serving in the local church for many years, I had the honor of working with many young adults as an academic dean of a Bible college. One thing was for certain, working with young adults had its many moments of carnality and immaturity. It wasn't their fault; they were just learning to control their flesh and everything else.

Developing into maturity is a process and it ultimately means not living by your feelings, moods, and childish reasonings. It means we *put away childish attitudes* **and** *behavior,* like strife, envying and divisions, and we walk in the love of God. (Romans 5:5). Spiritual babies are still controlled by their own desires and display selfishness in their walk. Instead of looking to God to help them and putting their trust in Him, they stir up conflict in the natural to get attention and control until their flesh is gratified. Spiritual babies want to be seen, cry loudly, to be heard and seek to manipulate others to get their own way. Proverbs 28:25 declares, *"He that is of a proud heart stirreth up strife: but he that has TRUST IN THE LORD SHALL BE MADE FAT."* The New English Bible declares, *"A self-important man provokes quarrels, but he who trusts in the Lord grows fat and prosperous."*

In 1 Corinthians 3:1-3, we catch a perfect illustration of those not developed in the love walk yet. *"And I brethren, could not speak unto you as spiritual, but as unto carnal, even as babies in Christ. I feed you with milk, and not with meat for hitherto ye were not able to bear it, neither yet now are you able. For ye are yet CARNAL, for whereas there is among you ENVYING, and STRIFE, and DIVISIONS, are ye not carnal and walk as men."* The Knox Translation of 1 Corinthians 3:1 declares, *"... and when I preached to you, I had to approach you as men with natural thoughts, YOU WERE LIKE LITTLE CHILDREN IN CHRIST'S NURSERY."*

Have you ever noticed that where selfishness is operative, strife is always near? God forbid that the last days church of the Lord Jesus Christ be filled with spiritually old, under-developed babies. It's one thing to have a bad moment, it's another thing to operate with malice, and cause trouble for God-appointed leadership for self-gain.

Romans 16:17-18 declares, *"Now I beseech you, brethren, MARK THEM WHICH CAUSE DIVISIONS contrary to the doctrine which you have learned; and avoid them. For they that are such serve not our Lord Jesus Christ, but their own belly; and by GOOD WORDS AND FAIR SPEECH deceive the hearts of the simple."* The Hudson Translation declares, *"... people like these are not serving our Lord Christ, but their own interests."*

Thank God this is the exceptional problem to the majority that genuinely loves God with all their hearts and serves Him faithfully. Granted, we will always have an inflow of new Christians being brought into the Kingdom of God, but to be born again for many years, and still holding onto childish actions should not be. We must always thank God for His unconditional love to continue to work with all His sons and daughters. Philippians 1:6, declares, ***"Being confident of this very thing, that he which hath begun a good work in you will perform it until the day of Christ Jesus."***

Let's determine to work out our salvation with fear and trembling before God, and live free from selfishness and walk in love. When we get our eyes off ourselves in these last days to assist God's leaders to obey the mandate to reach the world with the gospel, we will find fulfillment in life.

GET DELIVERED FROM THE "GREENER GRASS" SCENARIO

The devil will do everything he can to tell you that the season that you're in now is not exciting and there is something bigger for you, if you could just get to the next place. The reality is this, God may have greater responsibility awaiting you, but *"the grass needs to be mowed over there, too."* Why not settle down, be faithful, work hard, and give your best each day. Trust in God to help you grow and overcome where you are right now. If you cannot master the season you're in now, what makes you think you're ready for the next season? "If you cannot *develop peace* with God in your *now season*, surely your *tomorrow season* will defeat you also."

God desires us to trust Him and cast our care upon Him right where we are. He will help us through. In 1 Corinthians 15:58 it declares, ***"Therefore my beloved brethren, be ye steadfast, unmovable, always abounding in the WORK OF THE LORD, for as much as ye know that your labour IS NOT IN VAIN IN GOD."*** Then Galatians 6:9 declares, ***"And let us not BE WEARY IN WELL DOING: for in due season WE SHALL REAP, if we FAINT NOT."*** The truth is, when we do not grow weary, but continue to obey God, we are making progress and exhibiting faithfulness in our lives unto God and man.

The devil is the author of the "greener grass" scenario. He wasn't settled with his position in heaven, so he got pushy and went looking for another one. Unfortunately, he picked the wrong person to try to undermine, Jesus. What was the end result of his self-delusion and deception—total separation from God's presence and eternal damnation. Satan was no longer welcome in the presence of God. Jesus defined this actual moment in Luke 10:18, *"And he said unto them, I beheld Satan as lighting fall from heaven."*

If you're in a season right now where you're starting to feel restless and discontent and you know God has still called you there, Satan may be pushing your button. He may be putting lies in your thought life to persuade you to stop trusting God. He may be attempting to disconnect you from God's will and those in your life, over you in authority, who are doing their best to follow His will.

Psalm 46:10 declares, *"Be still and know that I am God."* Maybe you're feeling disconnected because you haven't totally embraced the season God has designed for you. Or maybe you feel like you haven't been fully embraced by those in authority. If you are wise, you'll just walk humbly before God and man, allowing God to lift you up. Don't be so concerned with others recognizing your calling or not, just serve and love people around you. God will take care of you and see to it you do all His will. Faithfulness means, whatever, and wherever God has called us to be and do, we willingly submit ourselves, trusting God always. Determine right now to give your best to God in the season you're in. He will strengthen and grace you to continue to grow in faithfulness for all that is ahead in His plan.

HAVE A THANKFUL HEART

You might not be where you want to be, but remember, you're not where you used to be. God has blessed you and done many wonderful things in your life to even bring you to this point. Don't be ungrateful by taking for granted the many blessings He has allowed you to partake of. In 1 Thessalonians 5:18 it declares, *"IN EVERYTHING GIVE THANKS: for this is the will of God in Christ Jesus concerning you."* The Message Bible declares*, "Be cheerful all the time."* Learn to appreciate each day and the privilege you have to serve God and someone else. Webster's dictionary defines ***thankful*** as: ***grateful; having an expression of gratitude, or appreciative.***

Remember, life is a whole lot easier when you maintain a thankful disposition anyway. If you have a job, be thankful. If you have a home and a car, be thankful. If you have the privilege to serve in the local church, count it an honor. If you have wonderful children, be thankful. If you have your health, be thankful. If you have a husband or wife that is a blessing to you, be thankful. If you have breath today, be thankful. If you have received Jesus as your personal Savior and missed eternal damnation, be thankful. The list goes on and on!

Don't walk around with a chip on your shoulder, thinking the world owes you something. Nobody owes you anything. That's not the proper attitude of a faithful servant of God. Determine you're going to take each day as an opportunity to make your life count unto God. Don't settle for anything less than what God's Word declares. The doorway of blessing is open to all! Stop right now and reevaluate all that God has given you and thank Him. There is just no place for feeling sorry for yourself when God has done so much already for you. As the old saying goes, ***"count your blessings!"***

Chapter 6

DIVINELY DESIGNED TO HAVE DOMINION

"And from the days of John the Baptist until now the kingdom of heaven suffereth violence, and the violent take it by force" (Matthew 11:12).

"In Christ we become God's sons, man's servants and the devils master."
—John G. Lake

"Do not imprison Christ in you. Let him live, let him manifest himself. Let him vent through you."
—John G. Lake

"Any man can be a master over the devil overnight."
—F.F. Bosworth

Dominion. What a powerful word. To dominate, to rule, to master—it defines the image of one who cannot be subdued, but subdues all. Webster's dictionary says ***dominion*** means: ***supreme authority, to rule, or to govern in a territory.*** Do you realize that this is exactly what God created mankind for? In Genesis 1:26 we read, **"Then God said let us make man someone like ourselves to be masters of all life upon the earth"** (The Living Bible). The Amplified Bible declares God granted to us, **"… COMPLETE AUTHORITY in the earth … over the fish of the sea, the fowl of the air, over every creeping thing."**

God, the ultimate Master, made us in His image—masters of all life upon the earth. We were fashioned as His highest creation, just underneath Himself. Psalm 8:4-6 reveals the high esteem God placed upon mankind.

"What is man that You are mindful of him, and the son of man that You visit him? For You have made him a little lower than the angels, and You have crowned him with glory and honor. You have made him to HAVE DOMINION over the works of your hands; You have put all things under his feet ..." (NKJV). Now, whose idea was it for us to have dominion? It was God's idea! He made us with the intention of us ruling and governing His creation.

The word translated "angel" in the above passage is the Hebrew word "Elohim," which most references tell us actually means "God." In other words, God fashioned us a little lower than Himself. A more correct rendering would read, **"For Thou hast made him but a little lower than God and crowned him with glory and honor"** (Berkley's Translation). This is YOU we're talking about!

But man's dominion was interrupted. Satan, in the form of a serpent, deceived Eve into disobeying God. Adam followed her lead and also disobeyed God's command to not eat of the tree of the knowledge of good and evil. With that act of defiance, the authority that Adam and Eve had over God's works was handed over to the devil. (Genesis 3:1-6).

Instantly man fell from the presence of God, forfeited the glory and became the victim of spiritual death with Satan now being the lord over the earth. Dominion changed hands … from Adam to the devil. And with the loss of dominion, the sin nature entered the race of men.

But God did not leave us in our fallen state. He raised up the Redeemer, Jesus Christ, to buy us back and restore proper order! *"For if by one man's offense death reigned through the one, much more those who receive abundance of grace and of the gift of righteousness will reign in life through the One, Jesus Christ"* (Romans 5:17, NKJV). The Living Bible declares, **"Adam caused many to be sinners because he disobeyed God and Christ caused many to be made accepted to God because He obeyed."** God's great plan of redemption reinstated mankind back to spiritual life and his place of authority.

Through Jesus Christ, God recreated a master race of sons and daughters who have His nature of love reborn in their spirits, who dominate the devil and the passions and desires of sinful flesh. *"Therefore, if anyone is in Christ, he is a new creation; old things have passed away; behold all things have become new"* (2 Corinthians 5:17).

The Cotton Patch Translation states it this way, *"Therefore if a man is a Christian, he is a brand new creation. The old guy is gone, a new man has appeared."* The Living Bible states, *"When a man becomes a Christian, he becomes brand new inside. He is not the same anymore. A new life has begun."*

We are divinely designed to live in dominion. As a new Creation, man and woman, we have dominion over the devil, over sin, failure and the past. God has now restored man to his original position of authority—walk like it, talk like it, and act like it! Let the following new creation facts encourage you to take your place of dominion in Christ Jesus!

DOMINION OVER SATAN AND FALLEN EVIL SPIRITS

Spiritual forces are still the mightiest forces on the earth. They live in the midst of us. We must remember that through our regained position we are no longer under the control of Satan or his cohorts. We do not have to obey them. We must always remember when dealing with Satan and evil spirits that we are dealing with dethroned powers. Jesus now lives in us and by the power of the indwelling Holy Spirit and the authority of God's Word, we are masters over Satan and the evil forces around us. (1 John 4:4). F.F. Bosworth, author of *Christ the Healer*, once said, *"Anyone can become a master over the devil overnight."* We must exercise our dominion and authority in Christ.

Jesus made it clear that through Him, His church was to wreak havoc on the devil. *"And Jesus came and spoke to them, saying, 'All authority has been given to Me in heaven and on earth. GO THEREFORE and make disciples of all the nations, baptizing them in the name of the Father and of the Son and of the Holy Spirit ...'"* (Matthew 28:18-19, NKJV). We've been commissioned to go in His authority and power! Jesus said in Luke 10:19, *"BEHOLD, I GIVE YOU AUTHORITY to trample on serpents and scorpions, and OVER ALL THE POWER OF THE ENEMY, and nothing shall by any means hurt you"* (Luke 10:19, NKJV). You are no longer Satan's slave. You have dominion over the power of the enemy through the name of Jesus. (James 4:7, Ephesians 4:27).

DOMINION OVER SIN

When God made us new creations in Christ our spirits received the very life of God. Our nature was changed, and our bodies became the very temple of the Holy Spirit. (2 Corinthians 6:17-19). The sin nature, or spiritual death, that Adam and Eve invited into their hearts, that was passed on to every man, woman and child, no longer lives within us. Jesus has delivered us out of spiritual death and into eternal life. We are now the habitation of God. We are possessors of eternal life in this life. The very substance of His nature now lives in us. Now all we have to do is renew our mind to the Word of God and control the outward man, which is our flesh. Sin consciousness leaves when we see ourselves in Christ and renew our minds. (Roman 12:1-2). We have not yet received a glorified body, but that day will come when He returns. (1 Corinthians 15:51-58).

Romans 6:14 declares, *"For sin shall not have dominion over you, for you are not under law but under grace"* (NKJV). The Conybeare Translation states, *"... For sin shall not have mastery over you."* The Goodspeed Translation states, *"... Sin must no longer control you."* In other words, we are empowered from the inside by the Holy Spirit and the Word of God to resist and overcome the temptations of this life. We are no longer trying on our own to fulfill a list of rules. God has moved inside and brought with Him His nature, full of power, to conquer every work of darkness. If we do miss the mark and sin, God has made provision, *"If we confess our sins, He is faithful and just to forgive us our sins and to cleanse us from all unrighteousness"* (1 John 1:9, NKJV). We confess, He forgives, but the work continues—He wants to continuously drive out all unrighteousness from our thinking, so we can put on the new man, being renewed in the spirit of our mind. (Ephesian 4:23, Colossians 3:10).

DOMINION OVER SICKNESS AND DISEASE

God did not create us for sickness. Adam and Eve did not experience anything but God's health until they sinned against God and forfeited their dominion over Satan. When Satan became the lord of the earth, and a sin nature became a part of mankind, sickness and disease entered in on the scene. It had a right to dominate humanity. Through Christ, our restoration as sons and daughters of God has given us authority once again over sickness and disease.

Look at 1 Peter 2:24, speaking of Jesus, *"Who Himself bore our sins in His own body on the tree, that we, having died to sins, might live for righteousness—by whose stripes you were healed."* Another promise regarding healing is, *"'For I will RESTORE HEALTH TO YOU and HEAL YOU of your wounds,' says the Lord"* (Jeremiah 30:17, NKJV). And again, *"Beloved, I pray that you may prosper in all things and BE IN HEALTH, just as your soul prospers"* (3 John 1:2, NKJV).

It is time to exercise faith in God's Word concerning divine health. Sickness is our master no longer. In the name of Jesus we have authority over it. And remember not to consult with your senses or your circumstances, but esteem God's Word first and your senses will line up.

DOMINION OVER FEAR

Fear is no longer our master! *"For God has not given us a spirit of fear, but of power and of love and of a sound mind"* (2 Timothy 1:7, NKJV). Now, if God doesn't give fear, then who does? The devil. And if it is from the devil, no thank you! We're not dancing to his tune anymore.

What was the first thing Adam experienced when he disobeyed God? *"Then the Lord called to Adam and said to him, 'Where are you?' So he said, 'I heard Your voice in the garden, and I was AFRAID because I was naked; and I hid myself"* (Genesis 9:10, NKJV). The fall of mankind out of the protection and presence of God immediately produced fear. Fear is a direct byproduct of disobedience. But through the new birth, we are living a life that is longing to obey Him, not to gain His favor, but because He has already shown us favor.

Fear is a force just like faith. But we do not have to submit to it anymore. Fear paralyzes, faith empowers. *"Inasmuch then as the children have partaken of flesh and blood, He Himself likewise shared in the same, that through death He might destroy him who had the power of death, that is, the devil, and release those who through fear of death were all their lifetime subject to bondage"* (Hebrews 2:14-15).

When Jesus is our Lord, there is no longer a cause for fear, because we know in this life and the next, we have our life in Him. Satan no longer has the power to hold us in bondage through fear, unless we let him! Speak to the spirit of fear to go. Live free to obey God.

DOMINION OVER POVERTY AND LACK

God wants to be your source, your provider and supplier of all your needs. Through His principles of hard work, tithing and offerings toward the Gospel, we involve God in providing for us. Psalm 35:27 declares, **"... Let the Lord be magnified, WHO HAS PLEASURE IN THE PROSPERITY OF HIS SERVANT"** (NKJV). The Moffat's Translation states, **"... Who loves to see His servants prospering."** Jesus restored supernatural provision for God's sons and daughters.

Jesus paid a great price to provide for our physical as well as spiritual needs. **"For you know the grace of our Lord Jesus Christ, that though He was rich, yet for your sakes He became poor, that you through His poverty might become rich"** (2 Corinthians 8:9, NKJV). The Amplified Bible declares, **"... in order that by His poverty, you might become enriched—ABUNDANTLY SUPPLIED."**

Our part is to seek God first in every area of life, including our money, to prepare the way for Him to rebuke the devourer and provide for our needs. (Matthew 6:31-33, Malachi 3:10-11). When we determine to obey the Word of God with our tithes and offerings, we position ourselves for His provision. Poverty and lack have been broken through the death, burial and resurrection of Jesus; yet, if we do not tap into how prosperity is released, we will remain under its control. Do something today to release increase into your life by giving into the plan and will of God in the earth. We are divinely designed to have dominion!

Chapter 7

HEARING THE VOICE OF GOD

"To him the porter openeth; and the sheep HEAR HIS VOICE: and he calleth his own sheep by name, and LEADETH THEM OUT. And when he putteth forth his own sheep, he goeth before them, and the sheep FOLLOW HIM: for they KNOW HIS VOICE"
(John 10:3-4).

"The whole meaning of prayer is that we may know God."
—Oswald Chambers

"If you do all the talking when you pray, how will you ever hear God's answer?"
—A.W. Tozer

"God speaks in the silence of the heart. Listening is the beginning of prayer."
—Mother Teresa

Jesus promises us that once we become His children, He will lead us just as a shepherd leads his sheep. It is a comfort to know that God promises to not only go before us, but enable us to follow. He said we would clearly know His voice and understand what He is saying to us. It is very important for us to learn to develop a listening ear and a heart to obey.

Proverbs 20:27 reveals that it is in the spirit of man that the Holy Spirit leads us, *"The spirit of man is the candle of the Lord, searching all the inward parts of the belly."* The American Standard Translation declares, *"The spirit of man is the lamp of Jehovah, searching all his most innermost parts."* Never has there been a more important time for us to clearly hear what God is saying to us individually and as His Church, corporately.

In 1 Chronicles 12:32 we read that the sons of the tribe of Issachar were aware of the times in which they lived. They knew God's leadership for that day. *"And of the children of Issachar, which were men that had understanding of the times, to know what Israel ought to do ..."* The tribe of Issachar played a key role in the leadership of that day because they understood what God desired to do and knew the necessary steps to take to lead correctly. Psalm 37:23 declares, *"The steps of a good man are ordered by the Lord: and he delighteth in his way."*

If Israel could understand and follow the voice of God, then how much more should we, as Spirit-filled sons and daughters of God, hear His voice? How much more should we understand the hour in which we live? How much more should we follow His plans in the earth today?

Because God's Spirit lives in our hearts, we can know what He is saying and doing. We are in a new covenant established upon better promises. God is no longer on the outside! Our new birth in Christ has made us the dwelling place of God. *"What? Know ye not that your body is the temple of the Holy Ghost, WHICH IS IN YOU, which ye have of God, and ye are not your own"* (1 Corinthians 6:19). Christ abides in our hearts to lead, guide and manifest Himself to and through us.

God desires to reveal His good plan, not only for our present, but also our future. Jesus declared, *"Howbeit when he, the Spirit of truth, is come, he will guide you into all truth: for he shall not speak of himself; but whatsoever he shall hear, that shall he speak: and he will shew you things to come"* (John 16:13). The Message Bible declares, *"... He will not draw attention to himself: but will MAKE SENSE OUT OF WHAT IS ABOUT TO HAPPEN ... he will honor me, he will TAKE FROM ME and DELIVER IT TO YOU."*

One of the Holy Spirit's assignments is to *convey, announce* **and** *declare* to us God's heart. Let's expect His leading and delight in hearing His plans for us. If we will do so, we will avoid a lot of mistakes and accurately *"hit the mark."* Consider the following nuggets on the subject of hearing God's voice.

LISTEN TO YOUR HEART

God lives in our spirit or heart. Have you ever been at a crossroads? In your natural thinking, all signs were pointing in one direction, but your heart was telling you to take another course. Proverbs 3:5-6 declares, **"Trust in the Lord with ALL THINE HEART; and lean unto thine OWN UNDERSTANDING. In all thy ways acknowledge Him, and He shall direct thy paths."** When we are whole-heartedly seeking God, God speaks to our hearts. Since He lives on the inside, He speaks on the inside. We find safety as we follow His direction on the inside.

In 1 Thessalonians 5:23, the Apostle Paul defines man as a tri-union being, **"And the very God of peace sanctify you wholly; and I pray your whole SPIRIT and SOUL and BODY be preserved blameless until the coming of our Lord Jesus Christ."** According to the scripture, man is a spirit being, he possesses a soul, his mind, will and emotions, and he has a physical body. One minister said it this way, **"The spirit of man contacts the spiritual realm, the soul of man contacts the intellectual realm and the physical man contacts the natural realm."** We must always remember that God is a Spirit, and the way He contacts man is through our spirit by the power of the Holy Spirit within us. In John 4:24 Jesus said, **"GOD IS A SPIRIT: and they that worship him must worship him in spirit and in truth."** It is the indwelling Spirit of God that speaks to our spirit to lead and instruct our everyday lives.

Romans 8:14 declares, **"For as many as are LED BY THE SPIRIT OF GOD, they are the sons of God."** The Knox Translation states, **"Those who follow the leading of God's Spirit are all God's sons."** We need a listening ear to hear all the Spirit of God is communicating to us. All of God's sons and daughters should expect to be led by God's Spirit in their hearts.

LET PEACE MAKE THE CALL

Following God's Spirit means following God's peace. His peace should rule in our hearts. When we learn to follow after peace, we will make the right decisions. As a rule of thumb, if you do not have peace on the inside concerning any decision, then do not proceed. **"And let the peace of God rule in your hearts, to the which also ye are called in one body; and be ye thankful"** (Colossians 3:15). The Twentieth Century Translation states, **"Let the PEACE that Christ gives DECIDE all doubts within** *your hearts."* The Weymouth Translation declares, *"Let the peace of God ... settle all questions ..."*

The Amplified Bible states, *"And let the peace (soul harmony which comes) from Christ rule (act as umpire continually) in your hearts-deciding and settling with finality all questions that arise in your minds ..."* If God's peace is our constant umpire, we will hear the correct calls and follow Him in both small and big things. It's so important that we do not violate what our heart is trying to communicate to us from God.

In Romans 9:1, we can see the relationship between our conscience and the Holy Spirit living within, *"I say the truth in Christ, I lie not, MY CONSCIENSE ALSO BEARING WITNESS IN THE HOLY GHOST."* Our conscience is the voice of our recreated born-again spirit. According to the scripture, our spirit has the capacity to fellowship with the Holy Spirit, bearing of God's leading to our spirit. When we listen to the witness of the Holy Spirit within, our conscience then communicates to our intellect God's leadership for our lives. When we choose to obey the witness of the Holy Spirit in our spirit, we can be sure that we are following Gods leadership. When we reject to listen and disobey, great regrets follow. In 1 Timothy 1:19, it declares, *"Holding faith and a GOOD CONSCIENCE; WHICH SOME HAVE PUT AWAY concerning faith and HAVE MADE SHIPWRECK."*

When we step away from obedience to the Word of God and fail to listen to our conscience, we are a ship off course, heading for the rocks of regret and harm. Albert Einstein once said, *"Never do anything against conscience even if the state demands it."* Billy Graham once said, *"Most of us follow our conscience as we follow a wheelbarrow. We push it in front of us in the direction we want to go."* Martin Luther said, *"It is neither safe nor prudent to do anything against conscience."* The good news is, we can follow the inward witness from within our spirit and let the peace of God on the inside make the call!

PRAYING IN THE SPIRIT

Praying in the Holy Spirit is a tremendous pipeline to God. Ephesians 6:18 encourages us, *"Praying always with all prayer and supplication IN THE SPIRIT, and watching thereunto with all perseverance and supplication for all saints."* The Taylor's Translation states we should be, *"Praying all the time, asking God for anything in line with the Holy Ghost's wishes."* The New English Bible declares, *"Give yourselves to prayer and entreaty, praying on every occasion in the power of the Spirit."*

There are great benefits to the baptism of the Holy Spirit and praying in other tongues. Praying in the Spirit is the doorway into the supernatural power of God and His leadings. It is through praying in the Spirit that we are built up in our hearts. We position ourselves to hear God's voice with great clarity. (1 Corinthians 14:4). In this place of prayer, the Holy Spirit speaks deep within our hearts, telling us all that pertains to life and godliness. (2 Peter 1:4).

In 1 Corinthians 2:9-10,12, we see that God reveals things to us by the Holy Spirit, *"But as it is written, EYE HATH NOT SEEN, NOR EAR HEARD, NEITHER HAVE ENTERED THE HEART OF MAN, THE THINGS WHICH GOD HATH PREPARED FOR THEM THAT LOVE HIM. But God hath REVEALED THEM UNTO US BY HIS SPIRIT: for the Spirit searcheth all things, yea, the deep things of God … Now we have received, not the spirit of the world, but the spirit which is of God; THAT WE MIGHT KNOW THE THINGS FREELY GIVEN TO US FROM GOD."*

There are specific things that God has prepared for all His children that we will not apprehend until we take time to pray in the Spirit. It is out of this place of prayer, that we will know those things that are freely given to us from God. We are called to set aside time each day to commune with the Holy Spirit to tap over into the deeper things of God's heart for our lives. Praying in tongues will prepare our hearts to receive instruction from God and create within us a greater sensitivity to the Holy Spirit's leading.

We must tap into God's leading by spending time praying in the power of the Holy Spirit! In 2 Corinthians 13:14, from the Phillips Translation, it exhorts us to have special times of fellowship with the Holy Spirit. *"The grace of the Lord Jesus Christ, the love of God, and the FELLOWSHIP that is ours in the HOLY SPIRIT be with you all"* (2 Corinthians 13:14). The King James declares, *"… and THE COMMUNION OF THE HOLY GHOST, BE WITH YOU ALL. Amen."*

MEDITATE ON THE WORD

God's Spirit will always lead us directly in line with the Word. Many times we ask God for direction that is already plain and clear in the Word. If we get unction contrary to the Word of God, we should throw it out! God never contradicts His Word. Joshua 1:8 declares, *"This book of the law shall not depart out of thy mouth; but thou shalt meditate therein day and night, that thou mayest observe to do according to all that is written therein: for then thou shalt make thy way prosperous, and then thou shalt have good success."*

We must give ourselves to study, rightfully dividing the Word on all matters of life. At all times we must ask ourselves, "What does the Word have to say concerning my situation?" We will walk in perfect freedom in Christ Jesus when we line ourselves up with His Word. Proverbs 4:20-22 encourages us, *"My sons, ATTEND TO MY WORDS; incline THINE EAR UNTO MY SAYINGS. Let them not depart from thine eyes; KEEP THEM IN THE MIDST OF THINE HEART. For they are life unto those that FIND THEM, and health to all their flesh."* We will never follow God fully if we do not know the counsel of His Word.

David exhorted us along these lines in Psalm 51:6, *"Behold, thou DESIRETH TRUTH IN THE INWARD PARTS: and in the hidden part thou shalt make me know wisdom."* God desires His Word to live in our spirits. In this we will walk not in our own way, but in God's paths of wisdom. God is pleased with sincerity of heart, but also sincerity mixed with understanding. Psalm 119:133 declares, *"ORDER MY STEPS IN THY WORD: and let not any iniquity have dominion over me."* Then in Psalm 119:130 declares, *"The ENTRANCE OF THY WORDS GIVETH LIGHT; it giveth understanding unto the simple."*

Follow the Word of God and you will walk into God's blessing, protection and direction for your life. Psalm 119:105 states, *"Thy word is a LAMP UNTO MY FEET, AND A LIGHT UNTO MY PATH."*

CONFESS YOU HEAR HIS VOICE

Over the many years of travel and working in the local church, I have come across many individuals who confess that they can't seem to hear God's voice. I learned early on in my Christian walk, to confess that I always hear God's voice and that He is always speaking clearly in my heart every day. That wasn't to convince God to do it; it was to build my expectation in what God was already doing—talking to my heart. Proverbs 23:15-16 declares, *"My son, if thine heart be wise, my heart shall rejoice, even mine. Yea, my reins shall rejoice, when thy lips speak right things."* The New Century Translation states, *"I will be so pleased IF YOU SPEAK WHAT IS RIGHT."*

God declares His sheep hear His voice. If He says it, then we would be wise to believe and talk in line with it. Start right now saying, *"I hear God's voice clearly. His Word and Spirit are always leading me into all truth."* Get negative communication out and start speaking God's Word over your life. Learn the language of victory, which is faith in Christ on your lips. Romans 10:8 declares, *"But what saith it? The word is nigh thee, even in thy mouth, and in thy heart: that is, the word of faith, which we preach."*

Our words chart our course, frame our world and determine our success or failure. Hebrews 11:3 declares, *"Through faith we understand that the worlds were FRAMED BY THE WORD OF GOD …"* Let's frame our world with God's Word. The more we confess the Word, the greater its truth will register in our spirits. You hear God's voice. You are on speaking terms with the Almighty.

DISTANCE YOURSELF FROM DISTRACTIONS

The high-tech world we live in today targets our senses with all sorts of information. What we expose ourselves to will either distract and hinder or help us hear God clearly. In 1 Corinthians 14:10 it declares, *"There are, it may be, SO MANY KINDS OF VOICES IN THE WORLD, and none of them is without signification."* With each voice, comes some type of persuasion. Every persuasion has an agenda.

Satan is roaring, doing all he can to get our attention onto circumstances, to steal our attention away from God. In Galatians 5:7-8 we find one of Satan's strategies is to disrupt our progress though false teaching. *"Ye did run well; who did hinder you that ye should not obey the truth? This PERSUASION COMETH NOT OF HIM THAT CALLETH YOU. A little leaven leaveneth the whole lump."*

When we close the door to the devil's influence and open our hearts and minds to the Lord, we will hear and follow God's voice. James 4:7 declares, *"Submit yourselves therefore to God. RESIST THE DEVIL, and he will flee from you."* The Twentieth Century Translation states, *"... and give no opportunity to the devil."* The New English Bible states, *"... leave no loop-hole for the devil."* We will better hear God's voice when we protect our environment from the devil's influences. Proverbs 4:23 admonishes us, *"Keep thy heart with all diligence; for out of it are the issues of life."* We can cultivate sharp hearing by "feeding" on the right things—the things of God!

GET ALONE WITH GOD

If we want to be close with God, we must take special time alone with Him. Even in natural relationships, if you want to get to know someone better, time with them is a must. In Luke 18:1, Jesus exhorts us, *"And he spake a parable unto them to this end, THAT MEN OUGHT ALWAYS TO PRAY, and not to faint."* The William's Translation states, *"How necessary it is for people always to pray." Prayer in its simplest definition is "talking to God."*

Effective communication is two-fold—*talking* **and** *listening*. James 4:8 declares, *"DRAW NIGH TO GOD, AND HE WILL DRAW NIGH TO YOU."* When we step toward God, we find He is eager to step toward us. When we pursue God, He in turn, responds to us. *"But it is good for me to DRAW NEAR TO GOD: I have put my trust in the Lord God, that I may declare all thy works"* (Psalm 73:28).

Jesus' example was constant fellowship with the Father: *"And he (Jesus) withdrew himself into the wilderness, and prayed;"* ... *"But he often would slip away and pray"* (NAS); *"He however, HABITUALLY WITHDREW TO PRAY"* (Luke 5:16, Berkley Translation). In Luke 6:12 we find Jesus again committing Himself to prayer, *"And it came to pass in those days, that he went out into a mountain to pray, and CONTINUED ALL NIGHT IN PRAYER TO GOD."* This is the place of power. This is the place of comfort. This is the place of direction. Let's press in for more of God. His purposes and plans are all for our taking. You are His child, and you can hear His voice!

Chapter 8

THE PLACE OF ABIDING

*"If ye abide in me, and my words abide in you,
ye shall ask what ye will, and it shall be done unto you"*
(John 15:7).

*"If you want that splendid power of prayer, you must remain
in loving, living, lasting, conscious, practical, abiding union
with the Lord Jesus Christ."*
—C.H. Spurgeon

*"There is no condition of life in which we cannot abide in Jesus;
we have to learn to abide in Him wherever we are placed,
our brilliant heritage."*
—Oswald Chambers

When we receive Jesus Christ as Savior and Lord, the blessings and privileges of Heaven opened up to us. We became brand new creatures, Christ living in us and we in Him. We became partakers of His divine nature (2 Peter 1:4). One of the greatest blessings of being in Christ is the bold access we now have to come before and live before the very throne of God (2 Corinthians 5:17; Psalm 103:2, 68:19; Hebrews 4:16).

Even though Christ lives within us, and He is always with us, most of us are not keenly aware of Him. And yet, it is in the place of dependency and union with God's Word and Spirit that our lives spring forth with abundant fruitfulness. We cannot be like Jesus apart from our communion with Jesus. We want to bear the fruit of the life and ministry of Jesus without paying the price to abide in God's presence as He did. (Luke 5:16, Luke 6:12).

Jesus said, *"I am the vine, ye are the branches: He that ABIDETH IN ME, and I in him, the same bringeth forth MUCH FRUIT: for without Me ye can do nothing"* (John 15:5). It is the vine alone that brings the nourishment and life the branch needs to bear fruit. Severed from that vine, the branch will surely wither and die. Other translations of this verse say: ***"... whoever REMAINS IN UNION with Me and I in union with him will bear abundant fruit"*** —William's Translation; ***"When you're joined with Me and I with you, the relation intimate and organic, THE HARVEST is sure to be abundant. Separated, you can't produce a thing"*** (MSG).

We often emphasis, as we should, the need for revival in the church and the abundant harvest of souls in the last days. But without habitual fellowship with God we will not carry the presence of God to even fulfill such a task. It is in the place of abiding that we reproduce the same fruitfulness of the life and ministry of Jesus. The American College dictionary defines *abide* as: *to remain, to continue in a certain condition or place, to stay in or dwell.* And this is what Jesus calls us to do in Him.

Jesus is looking for us to cultivate our relationship with Him. James 4:8 declares, ***"DRAW NIGH TO GOD, and HE WILL DRAW NIGH TO YOU."*** Many of us are trying to pick out the rocks, sticks and weeds from our own lives, and we're exhausting ourselves in the process. Jesus is the only One Who is able, and He calls us to abide in Him, to open up to Him, to stay in Him, so that the intense work of cultivation can begin. Our effort is in the coming, the submitting and the abiding. And Jesus promises to bring forth much fruit. In 1 Corinthians 1:9 it states, ***"God is faithful, by whom ye were CALLED UNTO THE FELLOWSHIP of His Son Jesus Christ our Lord."*** We need to answer that call to fellowship with Him. It is the place of transformation.

I played college football at the University of Buffalo as a wide receiver. In order to maximize my potential, I had to give myself one hundred percent to rigorous mental and physical discipline. I spent endless hours of disciplined weightlifting and running to prepare for the upcoming season. When game time came, I was able to perform and help contribute to the team's success. In our walk with Christ, so many of us are not even showing up for "practice." We're not yielding to the instruction of the Word of God and the coaching of the Spirit. We're not placing our lives into the hands of One Who is higher, with more victories under His belt; so that He can keep us close to train us up. We're launching out there into the "game of life" unprepared, frustrated, fatigued and failing. That's not the fruitfulness that Jesus promised we would bear if we would abide under His training (John 14:12, Acts 10:38, 1 John 3:8).

One unknown author said, *"It is not the mere touching of the flower by the bee that gathers the honey, but her abiding for a time on the flower that draws it out."* Have you been drawing out the life in Christ? Have you been abiding long enough that the nourishment and refreshment of His presence is flowing through you? Let's look at a few ways to abide in God.

ABIDING IN THE WORD OF TRUTH

Truth is powerful. Truth is a light in a dark place. The closer we walk in light of the Word of God, the less we trip and fall on obstacles around us. There is only one source of Truth—the Word of God. Jesus said, *"Thy Word is Truth"* (John 17:17). It is one thing to hear the truth; it is quite another to allow the truth to go deeper into our hearts and change us. The Apostle John said, *"For I rejoice greatly when brethren came and testified of the truth THAT IS IN YOU, just as you walk in the truth. I have no greater joy than to hear that my children WALK IN TRUTH"* (3 John 1:3-4, NKJV). The Message Bible declares, *"Nothing could make me happier than getting reports that my children CONTINUE diligently in THE WAY OF TRUTH."*

We must make decisions daily to continue in the way of truth. Jesus is demonstrated in our lives when we push past all opposition to live by the Word of God. Jesus said, *"If ye ABIDE in Me, and MY WORDS ABIDE in you, ye shall ask what ye will, and it shall done unto you"* (John 15:7). Jesus knows the power of truth working in our lives. If we are abiding in His Words, they will shape the innermost parts of who we are into His likeness. And out of His likeness, His truth, we ask what we will, and it is given to us.

We can see the dangers of straying from the truth when Jesus rebuked the Pharisees, *"You are of your father the devil, and the desires of your father you want to do. He was a murderer from the beginning, and does not stand in the truth, because there is no truth in him. When he speaks a lie, he speaks from his own resources, for he is a liar and the father of it"* (John 8:44, NKJV). The King James declares the devil *"... ABODE NOT in the truth."*

The devil's rebellion against the truth was His downfall. And he works tirelessly to distract us away from abiding in God's Word so that we will be susceptible to his lies. But fruitfulness in the Kingdom comes through abiding in the Word. (2 Timothy 2:15, Philippians 4:8, Proverbs 4:20, 21).

ABIDING IN PRAYER

Jesus often withdrew from the crowds to spend time with the Father. The Message Bible declares, ***"As OFTEN AS POSSIBLE Jesus WITHDREW to out-of-the-way places for PRAYER"*** (Luke 5:16). The result of that fellowship is found in verse 17, ***"And the power of the Lord was present to heal them."*** Jesus carried the yoke-destroying anointing because ***He abode in the place of prayer.***

James 5:16 states, ***"The earnest (heartfelt, continued) prayer of a righteous man makes TREMEDIOUS POWER AVALIBLE (dynamic is its working)"*** (AMP). The Message Bible states, ***"THE PRAYER OF A PERSON LIVING RIGHT WITH GOD IS SOMETHING POWERFUL TO BE RECKONED WITH."*** It is time to renew and strengthen our commitment to *abiding in prayer* with God. In Luke 6:12 we see the example of Jesus, ***"And it came to pass in those days, that He went out into a mountain to PRAY, and CONTINUED ALL NIGHT in prayer to God."*** Abiding prayer keeps us strong in the Lord and the power of His might (Ephesians 6:10). It means we not only pray, but we continue to pray. As we pour out our hearts to Him, He pours out Himself into us. We position ourselves to access the power and presence of God out of this place of abiding prayer.

ABIDING IN LOVE

Our love for God will drive us into the place of abiding in Him. And in response, the love that we find in Him will flow to the world around us. Compassion will compel us to meet the needs of those who are hurting and deprived of peace. Jesus declares, ***"As the Father hath loved Me, so have I loved you: CONTINUE YE IN MY LOVE. If ye keep My commandments, ye shall abide in love; even as I have kept my Father's*** *commandments, and ABIDE IN HIS LOVE. This is my commandment, that ye love one another, as I have loved you"* (John 15:9, 10, 12).

Love makes everything including our faith, work. Galatians 5:6 says, *"For in Jesus Christ neither circumcision availeth anything, nor uncircumcision; BUT FAITH WHICH WORKETH BY LOVE."* Look at these translations: *"... faith that finds its expression in love is all that matters"* —Knox Translation; *"... but only faith active in love"* —Moffatt Translation; *"... but only faith acting through love"*— Goodspeed Translation.

The ministry of Jesus is a ministry of compassion. Compassion drove Him to the harvest field. If we are not willing to develop in our love walk, to allow love to control our actions, we will not bear true fruit for the harvest. Matthew 9:36 declares, *"But when He saw the multitudes, He was MOVED WITH COMPASSION on them, because they fainted, and were scattered abroad, as sheep having no shepherd."*

In 1 Corinthians 13:4-8, it reminds us that no matter what we do or how noble it is, apart from a motive of love it is nothing. Let's look at a definition of love taken from the Message Bible:

... Love never gives up
... Love cares more for others than itself
... Love doesn't want what it doesn't have
... Love doesn't strut
... Love doesn't have a swelled head
... Love doesn't force itself on others
... Love isn't always me first
... Love doesn't fly off the handle
... Love doesn't keep score of the sins of others
... Love doesn't revel when others grovel
... Love takes pleasure in the flowering of truth
... Love puts up with anything
... Love trusts God always
... Love always looks for the best
... Love keeps going till the end

Wow! This is the way God loves us and wants to love others through us. Faith, hope and love will always endure, but the greatest of these is love (1 Corinthians 13:13). We can be trained to walk in love. By abiding in love, we keep the flesh crucified and the Lord exalted.

ABIDING IN FAITH'S CONFESSION

There is no real faith outside of believing and confessing the Word of God. Faith is activated in our lives when we believe God's Word as the final authority and declare all His blessings over our lives. Christianity finds its very roots in the confession of Jesus Christ as Lord and Savior. It was the very confession of His sacrifice on the cross that released you and me from the power of sin. The same ability to confess the Word over our lives will continue to keep us free from the law of sin and death. (Romans 8:2).

Confessing the Word of God over our lives releases our faith and moves the hand of God to watch over His Word to perform it. Proverbs 18:21 declares, **"DEATH AND LIFE ARE IN THE POWER OF THE TONGUE and they that love it shall eat the fruit there off."** When we fail to maintain a strong Word-based confession over every area of our lives, we have failed to abide in faith's confessions. Negative words, such as complaining and despair are only a result of stepping away from the Word of God. (Joshua 1:8).

Psalm 107:2, states, *"Let the redeemed of the Lord SAY SO, whom He hath redeemed from the hand of the enemy."* The Living Translation declares, *"… has the Lord redeemed you, then SPEAK IT OUT."* We are the redeemed of the Lord, and we have a lot to be excited about. When we discover who we are in Christ Jesus and what He has done for us through His death, burial and resurrection, we can't help but speak the Word of God. God has given us His Word for the purpose of targeting our faith. We must endeavor to train ourselves to have self-control where our words are concerned. Proverbs 23:16 declares, *"Yea my reins shall rejoice when thy LIPS SPEAK RIGHT THINGS."* The New Century Translation declares, *"I will be so pleased if you speak what is right."* *"… When your lips say right things,"* Basic American Standard Translation.

Jesus taught us in Mark 11:22-24, that faith has the ability to move mountains by the confession of our words. Yet, so many are all caught up in talking about how big their mountain is, rather than commanding it to move. Your mouth has the potential to change your circumstances or keep you trapped in them. When we choose to speak God's Word and continue in that place of strong Word confession, we are abiding for results. Hebrews 10:23 declares, *"Let us hold fast our profession of faith without wavering; (for He is faithful that promised;)."* The Twentieth Century Translation states, *"Let us maintain the confession of our hope unshaken, ... for He will not fail us."* Cotton Patch Translation declares, *"Let us hang on with tooth and toenail to our promising commitment, for He who maps our strategy can be completely trusted."* Determine today to maintain a strong faith confession that positions you for God's blessings to flow in your life.

ABIDING IN THE HOUSE OF GOD

We must never forget the Word of God directs us to attend church and to remain faithful in our attendance. Hebrews 10:25, from the Way Translation declares, *"LET US NOT ABANDON THE PRACTICE OF CHURCH GATHERINGS ... but use them as a means of mutual encouragement. Be all the more earnest in doing this, the nearer you perceive the day of the Lord to be."* The local church is God's plan for perfecting the saints for the work of the ministry. (Ephesians 4:8-11). It is the local church where you are pastored, the Word of God is taught, believers worship together and true relationships are established. In Luke 4:16, Jesus set an example for us to follow, *"So He (Jesus) came to Nazareth, where he had been brought up: and AS HIS CUSTOM WAS, He went into THE SYNAGOGUE ON THE SABBATH DAY, and stood up to read ..."* The New Living Bible states, *"... He went as usual to the synagogue."* The Message Bible declares, *"As He always did on the Sabbath, HE WENT TO THE MEETING PLACE."* Maintaining a regular commitment in attending church is a major key to a successful walk with God. It is out of the local church that the greatest days are ahead in God for the Body of Christ. Let's determine to submit and flourish in the house of God and be a blessing with our lives.

Chapter 9

WEATHERING THE STORMS WITHOUT BEING WEATHERED

*"And he shall speak words against the Most High [God] and shall **WEAR OUT THE SAINTS** of the **MOST HIGH GOD** and think to change the time [of sacred feasts and holy days]"*
(Daniel 7:25).

"Adversity causes some men to break and others to break records."
—William Arthur Ward

"Show me someone who has done something worthwhile, and I'll show you someone who has overcome adversity."
—Lou Holtz

Storms come and go. But one thing is certain; they do come. In 2 Timothy 3:12, it declares, **"Yea, and all that will live godly in Christ Jesus shall SUFFER PERSECUTIONS."** Since storms are inevitable, we better know not only how to weather them, but how to come out on top.

Why does it seem that when we make decisions to live godly, to apply the Word, that "*all hell breaks loose*?" Jesus told us why. He said, **"Afflictions and persecutions arise for the Word's sake"** (Mark 4:17). The Amplified Bible declares, **"Trouble or persecution arises on account of the Word."** The devil hates the Word of God. It is the very power that conquers him. So he stirs up trouble. He sends circumstances, people and problems our way to get us to let go of our faith! But Jesus declared us blessed even when persecuted, **"Blessed are they which are persecuted for righteousness' sake: for theirs is the kingdom of God"** (Matthew 5:10).

Just like a seed that is planted in the ground, the devil wants to uproot the truths of God's Word before they bear fruit in us. So don't be surprised by the challenges that come. Don't let the difficulties conquer you. Don't give your place of authority in Christ Jesus over to the devil by surrendering to the circumstances. In the midst of the raging storm, refuse to let go of God's Word, for He will not relax His hold on you.

You may be facing challenges even now as you read this book. My advice to you is to go back to the Word, pray through every assault of the devil, and remain true to God. Your victory will come. Peter wrote, ***"Beloved, THINK IT NOT STRANGE concerning the FIERY TRIAL that is to try you, as though some strange thing happened unto you: But rejoice, inasmuch as ye are partakers of Christ's sufferings"*** (1 Peter 4:12-13). The Amplified Bible, Classic Edition declares, ***"Beloved, do not be amazed and bewildered at the fiery ordeal which is taking place to TEST YOUR QUALITY, as though something strange—unusual and alien to you and your position—were befalling you."*** The Philip's Translation declares, ***"And now, dear friends of mine. Do not be unduly alarmed at the fiery ordeals which come to text your faith, as though they were some abnormal experience."***

Don't think it is odd when problems come—as though something must be wrong. It might well be because you are doing something right. The trouble could be there to get you to back off, to shut up, and to let go of the Word. This is a battle, not the Boy Scouts. In 2 Timothy 2:3, it declares, ***"Thou therefore ENDURE HARDNESS as a good soldier of Jesus Christ."*** The Message Bible declares, ***"When the going gets rough, take it on the chin with the rest of us, the way Jesus did."***

In 2 Corinthians 4:8-9, we see that conflicts come as a result of walking with God. ***"We are troubled on every side, yet not distressed; we are perplexed, but not in despair; persecuted, but not forsaken; cast down, but not destroyed."***

Other translations state, ***"Troubles are around us on every side, but we are not shut in"*** (Basic American Standard Translation). ***"We are persecuted, but we never have to stand alone"*** (Phillip's Translation). ***"Hunted down, but God never abandons us"*** (Taylor's Translation). ***"Always getting a knockdown, but never the knockout"*** (William's Translation).

God promised in His Word that He will never leave us in the midst of adversity but will always deliver us out into victory. Psalm 34:19 states,

"Many are the afflictions of the righteous: but the Lord delivereth him out of them all." The Amplified Bible declares, *"Many evils confront the consistently righteous, but the Lord delivers him out of them all."*

True, some problems in life are self-inflicted. But if you are facing adversity because you are seeking God's will and walking obediently, then it must be spiritual opposition. Ephesians 6:10-12 reminds us that we do not wrestle against flesh and blood, but spiritual powers. Remember that Satan comes; and he comes to steal, kill and destroy anything God is doing in our lives. But rejoice, because Jesus came to give us life that is abundant, overcoming. (John 10:10). Here are a few lifelines to help pull you through the storm.

DON'T BE SHOCKED

That's half the battle right there! According to the Word, difficulties and challenges are a part of the Christian walk. Job 5:7 declares, *"Man is born unto trouble, as the sparks fly upward."* Then in 1 Peter 4:12 we read, *"Dear friends, don't be bewildered or surprised when you go through the fiery trials ahead, for this is no strange, unusual thing that is going to happen to you"* (Living Bible Translation).

If you are not alert, you may think that something is wrong with you. Remember that we are, *"partakers of Christ's sufferings."* This is not suffering for Jesus with sickness, disease and fear. This is the suffering that comes from the devil's opposition to the Word of God alive in us.

Jesus constantly came up against the devil. He had opposition from ungodly and religious people. Just do as He did and keep on keeping on in what is right. You will weather the storm without it weathering you.

YOUR BATTLE IS NOT WITH FLESH AND BLOOD

Don't allow yourself to become confused by the vehicle trouble may come through. The Bible says we should not be ignorant of Satan's devices. (2 Corinthians 2:11). Spiritual attacks come from spiritual forces (Ephesians 6:10-12). Satan will try to bring trouble or storms to you through individuals who will yield to him to afflict you. We all have the choice as to whose instrument we will be. We're commanded, *"Neither yield your members as instruments of unrighteousness unto sin, but yield yourselves unto God ..."* (Romans 6:13).

Don't get entangled with people. Stay in the love of God. Pray for them and speak blessings over them. (1 Corinthians 13:4-8, 1 Peter 3:9, Romans 5:5). Refuse to fall into the devil's trap of handling things in the natural. Do battle God's way. You'll come out on top. Notice how Paul handled himself, *"Alexander the coppersmith DID ME MUCH EVIL: the Lord reward him according to his works"* (2 Timothy 4:14). In other words, Paul left Alexander's fate in God's hands. The New English Bible states, *"Retribution will fall upon him from the Lord."*

HOLD THE WHEEL AND STAY THE COURSE

A storm can easily change the course of a ship at sea. The captain must keep his hand on the wheel to keep it steady. If he lets go, the storm has won. *"Therefore, my beloved brethren, be ye STEADFAST, UNMOVABLE, always abounding in the work of the Lord, forasmuch as ye know that your labour is not in vain in the Lord"* (1 Corinthians 15:58). The Message Bible declares, *"Stand your ground and don't hold back. Throw yourself into the work of the Master."* The William's Translation declares *"... continue to be firm, INCAPABLE OF BEING MOVED."*

Don't let anything or anyone else direct your course contrary to the Lord and His Word. *"Submit yourselves therefore to God. Resist the devil, and he will flee from you"* (James 4:7). Keep yourself under God's hand. Do it His way all the time—when it's easy and when it's not. Your obedience resists and repels the devil.

KEEP YOUR COMPOSURE

Have you ever heard, "Don't panic; stay calm?!" Good advice. Things are rarely as bad as they seem, and the storm will pass you by. In 2 Corinthians 5:7, it reminds us that we *"walk by faith and not by sight."* The Twentieth Century Translation declares, *"For we guide our lives by faith, AND NOT WHAT WE SEE."* When we walk according to what we see, the storm can look too big to handle. But when we walk with the

Word of God as our final authority, then the storm has to blow over.

The Holy Spirit told Paul that bonds and afflictions awaited him in Jerusalem. But look at his attitude, *"But NONE OF THESE THINGS MOVE ME, neither count I my life dear unto myself, so that I might FINISH MY COURSE with joy, and the ministry, which I have received of the Lord Jesus, to testify the gospel of the grace of God"* (Acts 20:24). When the winds blow, we should say, *"None of these things move me."*

DON'T LOSE YOUR JOY

"THE JOY OF THE LORD is your strength" (Nehemiah 8:10). We only lose our joy when we stop trusting in the Lord. And when we lose our joy, we have surrendered our strength and succumb to defeat. Look at James 1:2-3, *"Dear Brothers, is your life full of difficulties and temptations? Then be happy (joyful), for when the way is rough, your patience has a chance to grow. So let it grow, and don't try to squirm out of your problems. For when your patience is finally in full bloom, then you will be ready for anything, full and complete"* (Living Bible Translation). Our joy is part of our recreated spirit. (Galatians 5:22). It is there always, no matter what. We just have to choose to walk in it, above the circumstances.

Look at the following quote, *"Afflictions come to the believer, not to make him sad, but sober; not to make him sorry, but wiser. Even as the plow enriches the field so that the seed is multiplied a thousandfold, so afflictions should magnify our joy and increase our spiritual harvest."*
—Howard Beecher

DRAW UPON THE STRENGTH OF GODLY ASSOCIATIONS

There should be individuals in your life that you know walk with God, that you can trust, who will stand with you. In difficult times, go to God first and appropriate His Word. Then find friends who can agree with you in prayer. (Matthew 18:19). True friends are God's idea. *"A friend loveth at all times and a BROTHER IS BORN FOR ADVERSITY"* (Proverbs 17:17). The Living Bible declares, *"A true friend is always loyal, and a brother is born to HELP IN TIME OF NEED."* A godly friend may have insight or revelation from God to aid and assist you. The last thing you want to do in a storm is rely upon those who have no experience successfully walking through one.

In 1 Corinthians 16:17-18 the Apostle Paul lists people who brought him godly and refreshing encouragement, ***"I am glad of the coming of Stephanas and Fortunatus and Achicus: for that which was lacking on your part they supplied. For they have REFRESHED MY SPIRIT AND YOURS: therefore acknowledge ye them as such."*** The Goodspeed Translation declares, ***"They have cheered my spirit and yours, too."*** The Conybeare Translation states, ***"for they have lightened my spirit and yours."***

LEARN THE LANGUAGE OF FAITH

Until you learn to master your lips, you will tumble every time in the face of adversity. Jesus' own disciples had to learn this very point. When they were caught in the midst of a storm, they panicked—even though Jesus was right there with them. ***"And, behold, there arose a great tempest in the sea, insomuch that the ship was covered with the waves: but He (Jesus) was asleep. And His disciples came to Him, and awoke Him, saying, 'Lord, save us: We perish.' And He saith unto them, 'Why are ye fearful, O ye of little faith?' Then he AROSE, AND REBUKED THE WINDS AND THE SEA; and there was a great calm"*** (Matthew 8:24-26).

Little faith will talk the problems, complain and yield the tongue to defeat. We need to trust Jesus; He is bigger than the problems, take our authority in His Name, and rebuke the circumstances that are in opposition to His Word! Take Jesus' example and speak to the storm, ***"Be still."*** Proverbs 18:21 declares, ***"DEATH AND LIFE are in the POWER OF THE TONGUE: and they that love it shall eat the fruit thereof."***

NEVER GIVE UP

Why does the devil bring storms? He does it to get us to give up our faith, to exhaust us in our believing. But be encouraged, for the Lord promises, ***"And let us not be weary in well-doing: for in due season we shall reap, if we faint not"*** (Galatians 6:9).

George Washington once said, *"Perseverance is one's duty."*

Martin Luther King, Jr. once said, *"The ultimate measure of a man is not found when a man stands in comfort or convenience, but where he stands in challenge and controversy."*

You would never face storms if you were no threat to the kingdom of darkness. And the fact that you are struggling against it means you have not been mastered by it! Never give up, but persevere and overcome. In 2 Corinthians 2:14, it reminds us, *"Now thanks be unto God, which ALWAYS CAUSETH US TO TRIUMPH IN CHRIST."* We must never give up no matter how difficult the situation may seem. God will not only stand with us, but also cause our stand of faith to turn the tables on adversity so that we will come out on the winning end!

You and I are never defeated—unless we give up. So face your adversity in the courage and strength of God, trusting Him to see you through. Nahum 1:7, states, *"The Lord is good, a STRONGHOLD IN THE DAY OF TROUBLE; and he knoweth them that TRUST IN HIM."*

Chapter 10

OVERCOMING SETBACKS

"So we must get rid of everything that SLOWS US DOWN, especially the sin that just won't do away and we must determine to run the race that is ahead of us"
(Hebrews 12:1, Contemporary English Version)

"Take us the foxes, THE LITTLE FOXES, THAT SPOIL THE VINES: for our vines have tender grapes"
(Song Of Solomon 2:15).

"Self-control is the quality that distinguishes the fittest to survive."
—George Bernard Shaw

"Before a man can bind the enemy, he must know there is nothing binding him."
—Smith Wigglesworth

These are the greatest days upon the face of the earth for the Body of Christ. God continues to move in such a spectacular way to confirm His Word with mighty demonstration and power. Yet, it is a sobering and serious hour for us as the Body of Christ. We must look within ourselves to see what is hindering us from advancing in the will of God and receiving all that God has in store.

The time has come to shed excess baggage and run the race God has set before us. Hebrews 12:1 declares**,** *"Wherefore seeing we also are compassed about with so great a cloud of witnesses, LET US LAY ASIDE EVERY WEIGHT, and the sin which doth so easily beset us, and let us RUN WITH PATIENCE THE RACE that is set before us."*

Some other translations declare:

"Let us lay aside every thing that hinders us" (Twentieth Century Translation)

"Let us rid ourselves of all that weighs us down" (Knox Translation).
"It means we better get on with it, strip down, start running and never quit" (MSG).

Smith Wigglesworth once said, *"The reason the world today is not seeing Jesus is because believers are not filled with the Spirit of Christ. They are satisfied with going to church occasionally and reading their Bibles sometimes. When God lays hold of us, there is then an end to the old self."*

A casual attitude toward the things of God will not do in the hour that we are living. The Word of God consistently exhorts the believer to pursue God and to live in His presence. We must keep God as our first priority, so we can hear from heaven and execute His will in the earth. The Greek word for weights *is ogkos,* which means, **heavy bulk, excessive weight, mass or heap.** Webster's dictionary defines *weight* as: **load, heaviness, burdens or that which obstructs or hinders us.**

In 1 Corinthians 11:23-33, the Apostle Paul teaches about the Lord's Supper, the great covenant that God has made with man. Through this ceremony we acknowledge His body, broken for our health and His blood, shed for a new, lasting covenant for all generations. In verses 28-31, we find Paul making a very important statement, *"But let a man EXAMINE HIMSELF and so let him eat of that bread and drink of that cup. For he that eateth and drinketh unworthily, eateth and drinketh damnation to himself, not discerning the Lord's body. For this cause many are weak and sickly among you and sleep (meaning death). For if we would JUDGE OURSELVES, we should not be judged."*

It is our responsibility to *examine* and *judge our lives* to see if our hearts are right before the Lord. Notice it didn't say we are to straighten everybody else out first, then straighten ourselves out. Many are too busy meddling in the lives of others, instead of minding their own business before the Lord. The key words are *examine* and *judge*. A healthy examination of our hearts before the Lord is a good thing and a biblical principal. We don't want to get in a ditch with this and allow Satan to put us under condemnation, either. (Romans 8:1-2, Romans 8:29). But we do need to maintain honest, heart-felt examinations before the Lord. These

translations contribute to our understanding of verse 28:
"Let him test himself" (Moffatt Translation).
"Have a self-examination" (Berkley Translation).
"Let each man look into his own heart" (TCNT).

The medical field offers annual checkups. The intention is to trouble shoot, to make sure the body remains healthy, and to head off any potential problems. The same must take place for the Body of Christ. We must examine ourselves to see if we are on the right course, remaining clear of preventable problems. I believe that the potential for great progress and achievement in the Body of Christ is just ahead. Yet, without honest evaluation, we may be carrying over into this year unnecessary baggage that will hinder us from experiencing revival in our hearts. So here are just a few things for you to think about as we press toward the mark of the high calling in Christ Jesus!

NEGATIVE COMMUNICATION

Until we learn to control the words of our mouth, we will be hindered and sidelined in God's plans. Proverbs 18:21 warns us, **"Death and life are in the power of the tongue: and they that love it shall eat the fruit thereof."** Knox's Translation says, **"Of life and death, the tongue holds the keys."** Our tongue will either bless or curse us. The Lord declares, **"I call heaven and earth to record this day against you, that I have set before you life and death, blessing and cursing: THEREFORE, CHOOSE LIFE, that both thou and thy seed may live"** (Deuteronomy 30:19).

Jesus told us, **"The words that I speak unto you, they are spirit, and they ARE LIFE"** (John 6:63). When we talk against the Word of God and complain about how bad things are we are setting into motion negative results. It is just as easy to speak the answers, as it is to complain about the problems. James 3:3-5 declares, **"Behold also the ship, which though they be so great, and are driven of fierce winds, yet are they turned about with a very small helm, whithersoever the governor listeth. Even so the tongue is a little member, and boasteth of great things. Behold how great a matter a little fire kindleth!"** According to the Word of God, our tongue is the rudder that directs our lives. The choice is ours every day which side of life we are going to live on. Let's choose faith-filled words and chart our course into God's best!

UNREPENTED SIN

This is not the hour to play around with sin. Through our new birth in Christ, our hearts have been remade in His image and the sin nature destroyed. But we still must harness our thoughts and control our flesh. (Romans 12:1-2). In the world we live in today, Satan is trying to saturate the minds of believers with impurity. The media, newsstands, movies, and music, have one agenda: to pursue and steal the affections of men and women away from God. Colossian 3:2 tells us to, *"Set your affections on things above, not on things of the earth." "You must be heavenly minded"* (Knox Translation); and *"Let heaven fill your thoughts"* (Living Bible Translation).

James 4:7 declares, *"Submit yourselves therefore to God. RESIST THE DEVIL, and he will flee from you."* Too many of us are resisting God and fleeing to the devil! We are seeing more and more reports about people getting hooked on internet pornography, infidelity in marriages, addictions to alcohol and cigarettes, and other the addictive behaviors of the mind and flesh. Why? Because too many of us are living open to whatever comes down the pike. In 2 Corinthians 6:17-18 the Word of God declares, *'"Wherefore COME OUT FROM AMONG THEM, AND BE YE SEPARATE,' saith the Lord, 'AND TOUCH NOT THE UNCLEAN THING; AND I WILL RECEIVE YOU, And will be a Father UNTO YOU, AND YE SHALL BE MY SONS AND DAUGHTERS, saith the Lord Almighty.'"* The Knox Translation declares, *'"Come out, then, from among them,' the Lord says to us, 'SEPARATE YOURSELVES from them, and DO NOT EVEN TOUCH WHAT IS UNCLEAN ..."'*

We must choose to go after God and turn away from sin. We are commanded to live a consecrated holy life unto God. We are further instructed, *"Have NO FELLOWSHIP WITH THE UNFRUITFUL WORKS OF DARKNESS, but rather reprove them,"* or *"Steer clear of the activities of darkness"* (Ephesians 5:11, Phillip's Translation).

Thank God as we are growing that His mercy is never changing and new every morning, and great is His faithfulness. (Lamentations 3:22-23).

If you have missed it, quickly run to God and ask Him to forgive you. In 1 John 1:9 it reminds us how, *"If we confess our sins, he is faithful and just to forgive us our sins, and to cleanse us from all unrighteousness."*

The Word of God will keep us pure and on the right track, as we meditate in it and keep it before our eyes. *"Wherewithal shall a young man cleanse his way? By taking heed thereto according to thy word. THY WORD HAVE I HID IN MINE HEART, that I might NOT SIN AGAINST THEE"* (Psalm 119:9, 11). Make a decision that you are not going to allow the little foxes to spoil the vine in your life, so you can walk unhindered in revival.

TOUCH NOT GOD'S ANOINTED

God calls us to honor and value the ministry gifts He has placed in our lives. Ephesians 4:11-12 declares, *"And he gave some, APOSTLES; and some, PROPHETS; and some EVANGELISTS; and some, PASTORS and TEACHERS; for the perfecting of the saints, for the work of the ministry, for the edifying of the body of Christ."* We don't fully understand the importance of honoring and respecting God's appointed leadership in our lives. In 1 Thessalonians 5:12-13 it declares, *"And we beseech you, therefore brethren, to know those that labour among you, and who are OVER YOU IN THE LORD and ESTEEM THEM VERY HIGHLY IN LOVE for their WORK SAKE. And be at peace among yourselves."*

When we esteem and honor the fivefold ministry gifts, we are honoring God in our lives. Failure to do so can result in much regret. The Message Bible declares, *"And now friends, we ask you to HONOR THOSE LEADERS WHO WORK SO HARD FOR YOU, who have been given the responsibility of urging and guiding you along in your obedience. OVERWHELM THEM WITH YOUR APPRECIATION AND LOVE."*

Many think nothing of talking negatively about leadership behind their backs. Many fail to see that ministry gifts were designed by God to grow us up in the knowledge of Him. The fivefold ministry gifts are not doormats for us to wipe our feet on, but God-appointed servants, who are anointed by His Spirit to help us. In 1 Timothy 5:17 it declares, *"GIVE DOUBLE HONOR TO SPIRITUAL LEADERS who handle* their duties well, this is especially true if they work hard at teaching the word of God" (God's Word Translation). The Living Bible declares, *"... Pastors who do their work well should be paid well and HIGHLY APPRECIATED and RESPECTED."* Our attitude toward the ministry gifts must only reflect honor and appreciation. It is dangerous ground to meddle with God's chosen servants.

"TOUCH NOT MINE ANOINTED and do my PROPHETS NO HARM" (Psalm 105:15). The P.K. Harrison Translation declares, *"LEAVE MY ANOINTED ONES ALONE; do not harm my prophets."* David, the author of this psalm, wrote directly out of his experience with the leadership in his life, King Saul. Even though Saul was in error and disobedient to God, David choice to keep his hands (and mouth) off of Saul. King Saul attempted to kill David 21 times. But when the tables were turned, and David had his chance to kill Saul in a cave, he refrained himself. In 1 Samuel 18:5 it declares, *"And David went out whithersoever Saul sent him and BEHAVED HIMSELF WISELY."* We need to behave wisely and not touch God's anointed. God will take care of it!

RECOGNIZE SELF APPOINTMENTED INDIVIDUALS—
INTOXICATED BY AMBITION

King David had 19 sons total. His third son, Absolom was David's favorite. He was the most handsome and gifted and no question in line for the throne of Israel. But his downfall was his pride. Proverb 16:18 declares, *"Pride goeth before destruction, and a haughty spirit before a fall."* The Message Bible declares, *"First pride, then the crash-the bigger the ego, the harder the fall."*

He would not stay submitted to his own father King David, who was GOD's Proven APPOINTMENT. Hebrews 13:17 declares, *"Obey them that have rule over you, and submit yourselves: for they watch over your souls, as they must give account, that they may do it with joy, and not with grief: for that would be unprofitable for you. "*

Absolom was ambitious and was eager to be the king. He wanted to be both seen and admired by men or Israel. Jeremiah 45:5 declares, *"And seekest thou great things for THYSELF? SEEK them NOT ..."* The

Living Bible declares, *"Are you seeking great things for YOURSELF? DON'T DO IT ..."*

As a result, he used his influence out of order to distort narratives to favor his influence against the real God-appointed leader, his Father. He used his influence in a shrewd and manipulative manner to actually steal the hearts of Israel away for the true God-appointment. His choice to exalt himself and his agenda led to a revolt against his father and drew the people away from the real God-appointed leadership.

He convoluted his leadership gift to promote himself and his own ego. The end result of his pride, reduced him to a mighty fall, which ultimately cost him his life.

3 TYPES OF APPOINTMENTS

There are three types of leadership appointments.
1. SELF appointment.
2. MAN'S appointments
3. GOD appointments.

The last is the right appointment and is very honorable in the eyes of GOD.

Be careful that you do not submit to the SELF and MAN'S appointment. They have giftings and talents, but if out of season are very dangerous to follow. They will lead you directly in opposition to real GOD-APPOINTED leadership. You will find yourself on the wrong side of God's order and headship.

These smooth-talking, self-appointments are very dangerous to listen to and wrong to follow. Examine their fruit and faithfulness. Do they sow division against real authority and pull peoples' hearts to their selfish ego narrative, or do they point people to God appointments and the Word of God with sincerity and to unity?

Do they exert their influence to sabotage real leadership by slandering them behind their backs, or unify people behind true Godly-appointed leadership?

Be wise and use discernment. Be careful who you listen to! There is always more to the story than what they present; they will use just enough information to sow discord and steal one's heart through gossip and slander behind the scenes! They talk one way publicly and another in private. And the real problem is they have never really submitted themselves to the real five-fold God appointments. Ephesians 4:11-16 declares,

> 11 "So Christ himself gave the apostles, the prophets, the evangelists, the pastors and teachers,
> 12 to equip his people for works of service, so that the body of Christ may be built up
> 13 until we all reach unity in the faith and in the knowledge of the Son of God and become mature, attaining to the whole measure of the fullness of Christ.
> 14 Then we will no longer be infants, tossed back and forth by the waves, and blown here and there by every wind of teaching and by the cunning and craftiness of people in their deceitful scheming.
> 15 Instead, speaking the truth in love, we will grow to become in every respect the mature body of him who is the head, that is, Christ.
> 16 From him the whole body, joined and held together by every supporting ligament, grows and builds itself up in love, as each part does its work."

SELF APPOINTMENTS LIFT UP THEMSELVES OVER THE CAUSE

We can see from the scriptures that Satan is the father of all self-appointment and exaltation. He was one of the three high, arch angels in heaven along with Gabriel and Michael. Lucifer was not content with his position and role in heaven. He wanted more and wanted to be the center of attention. Isaiah 14:12-15 proves this point clearly, ***"How art thou fallen from heaven, O Lucifer, son of the morning! how art thou cut down to the ground, which didst weaken the nations! For thou hast said in thine heart, I will ascend into heaven, I will exalt my throne above the stars of God: I will sit also upon the mount of the congregation, in the sides of the north: I will ascend above the heights of the clouds; I*** *will be like the most High. Yet thou shalt be brought down to hell, to the sides of the pit."*

It was actually Satan that mislead and STOLE the HEARTS of one third of the angels to lead a revolt against God and Jesus! Absolom's form of leadership is a direct pattern and example of Lucifer and what he attempted to do in heaven—that failed as well!

Lucifer was the pioneer of the first church split in heaven itself. But such arrogance and foolishness fails and the consequences for his rebellion and lack of submission was catastrophic to the human race!

Revelations 12:7-9 declares, *"And there was war in heaven: Michael and his angels fought against the dragon; and the dragon fought and his angels, And prevailed not; neither was their place found any more in heaven. And the great dragon was cast out, that old serpent, called the Devil, and Satan, which deceiveth the whole world: he was cast out into the earth, and his angels were cast out with him."*

Jesus gave account of this time in biblical history in Luke 10:18-20, *"And he said unto them, 'I beheld Satan as lightning fall from heaven. Behold, I give unto you power to tread on serpents and scorpions, and over all the power of the enemy: and nothing shall by any means hurt you. Notwithstanding in this rejoice not, that the spirits are subject unto you; but rather rejoice, because your names are written in heaven.'"*

LOOK FOR CHARACTER OVER CHARISMA

Charisma is built on personality, charm beauty, and personal qualities that are a gift from God. But character is built on integrity and moral values. Charisma is what people think we are, character is what we really are! Your character will only take you where you Charisma falters.

Proverbs 10:9 from the Living Bible Translation declares, *"People with integrity walk safely, but those who follow crooked paths will slip and fall."*

Proverbs 28:6 declares, *"Better is a poor man who walks in his integrity than a rich man who is crooked in his ways."*

Proverbs 11:3 declares, *"The integrity of the upright guides them, but the crookedness of the treacherous destroys them."*

Proverbs 20:7 declares, *"The Righteous who walk in his INTEGRITY—blessed are his children after him."*

1 Peter 2:12 declares, *"Keep your conduct among the gentiles HONORABLE, so that when the speak against you as evildoers, they may see your good deeds and glorify God on the day of visitation."*

GOD APPOINTMENTS UNIFY—SELF APPOINTMENTS BREED DIVISION

Romans 16:17 from the New International Version declares, *"I urge you, brothers and sisters, to watch out for those who cause divisions and put obstacles in your way that are contrary to the teaching you have learned. Keep away from them."*

New American Standard Bible declares, *"Now I urge you, brothers and sisters, keep your eye on those who cause dissensions and hindrances contrary to the teaching which you learned, and turn away from them."*

Weymouth New Testament declares, *"But I beseech you, brethren, to keep a watch on those who are causing the divisions among you, and are leading others into sin, in defiance of the instruction which you have received; and habitually to shun them."*

One other translation declares it this way, *"One final word of counsel, friends. Keep a sharp eye out for and mark those who take bits and pieces of the teaching that you learned and then use them to make trouble. Give these people a wide berth. They have no intention of living for or submitting their lives to our Master Christ. They're only in this to be seen for what they can get out of it, and aren't above using pious sweet talk and slick Willy words, to dupe unsuspecting innocents."*

Unfortunately, there are people operating under the influence of the Absolom spirit of self-promotion and self-exaltation. They are slick and dangerous. They very cunning and divisive. They will go to work and dismantle real God appointed leaders with behind the scenes through criticism and dishonor.

Their agenda is clear, to destroy in your mind those that are in authority, with an ultimate goal to replace them with their own influence in your heart and mind. They are deceptive and crafty and very dangerous. Ask yourself do they speak badly and divide or honorably unite? These rebellious spirits don't think anything of destroying God appointed leaders with divisive and controversial ideas and views. After all, if they were in authority they would not do it this way, just like ABSOLOM. In order to promote themselves, they have to dismantle others with their words and distorted Charisma. Avoid such manipulative people and stay submissive to real God appointed men.

WALKING IN OBEDIENCE

As I travel the United States, I talk with many, many pastors. I see a common trend in all of their churches—people problems. I am not talking about good people dealing with problems, and who are looking for answers. I am talking about people who struggle with submission issues and create all kinds of problems for God appointed leadership. No leader is perfect, but they are called, and they work very hard to obey God and help others. Be patient with them as they are with you.

Hebrews 13:17, declares, ***"OBEY THEM THAT HAVE RULE OVER YOU, AND SUBMIT YOURSELVES: for they watch over your souls, as they that must give an account, that they may do it with joy, and not with grief: for that is unprofitable to you."*** When we malign and slander God's appointed leaders we hinder ourselves. Psalm 17:3 declares, ***"I have purposed that my mouth shall not transgress."*** Pray for them as they obey the mandate upon their lives, church or ministry.

Be a help to leadership. Don't be high maintenance. Focus on being a servant and blessing. Those who are constantly criticizing and slandering leadership are the very ones who do not have Hebrews 13:17 working in their lives.

Revival is coming through the local church, which means God's appointed leadership. These ministry gifts will be the instruments to guide us into the best days we have ever seen in God. So, let's hook up and walk in obedience to God. Resist a critical attitude and flow under the blessings of the local church. Learn to respect and honor godly leaders, avoid the sin of familiarity, and God will bless you. (Matthew 13:55-57).

The true test of progress with God is seen in our level of obedience. Every step of obedience we take shows a deeper level of trust in Him.

Oswald Sanders once said, *"The golden rule for understanding in spiritual matters is not intellectual but obedience."* Corrie Ten Boon once said, *"When we are obedient, God will guide our steps and our stops."* J. Robert Ashcroft said, *"All of heaven is waiting to help those who will discover the will of God and obey."* When we refuse what God has spoken to us and commanded in His Word, we decline spiritually. We show that we trust ourselves more than the Lord. He is waiting to bless and help us when we are *obedient to His will.*

Webster's dictionary defines *obedience* as: **a *readiness to comply, excessive compliance, submission, due and willing submission to authority.*** In every arena of life, there are rules, regulations and laws, instituted to keep peace and safety. The wise seek to obey and those who don't suffer for it. Look at Isaiah 1:19-20, *"If ye be WILLING and OBEDIENT, ye shall eat the good of the land: But if you refuse and rebel, ye shall be devoured by the sword: for the mouth of the Lord has spoken it."* God's motivation in obedience is to keep us safely in His provision and care—out of the reach of destruction. *"Obedience is the burial of our will and the resurrection of humility."* —author unknown.

In Acts 26:19, we find the Apostle Paul appearing before King Agrippa, marking His commitment to the heavenly vision, which he received from God, *"Whereupon, O King A-grip-pa, I WAS NOT DISOBEDIENT TO THE HEAVENLY VISION."* The Twentieth Century Translation declares, *"I did not fail to obey the HEAVENLY VISION."* Determine you will remain faithful right where you are in life and obey what God is asking you to do and great rewards will follow.

TITHES AND OFFERINGS

The tithe is a tenth of our income. Offerings are anything given above the tithe. Tithes and offerings belong to God. Malachi 3:8-10 declares, *"Will a man rob God? Yet you have robbed me. But ye say, 'Wherein have we robbed thee?' IN TITHES AND OFFERINGS. Ye are cursed with a curse: for ye have robbed me, even this whole nation. 'Bring ye all the tithes into the storehouse, that there may be meat in my house, and prove me now herewith,' saith the Lord of hosts, 'If I will not open the windows of heaven, and pour you out a blessing, that there shall not be room enough to receive it.'"* When we fail to cooperate with God's Word, to bring the tithe and offering into His house, the local church, we hinder God's plan.

The Lord said we are cursed when we rob Him in tithes and offerings. It belongs to God, and if we trust Him, we know He only wants to bless our finances through our obedience. The tithe opens heaven's window, and the offering causes God's abundant supply to come our way. Remember, our harvest is in direct relationship to the seeds we sow. Galatians 6:7 declares, **"Be not deceived; God is not mocked: FOR WHAT SO EVER A MAN SOWEWTH, THAT SHALL HE REAP."** The Phillip's Translation declares, **"Don't be under any illusion, A MAN'S HARVEST IN LIFE will depend entirely on WHAT HE SOWS."**

God desires to teach us how to prosper. In 3 John 1:2 it declares, **"Beloved I wish above all things that THOU MAYEST PROSPER and be in good health, even as thy SOUL PROSPERETH."** When we accept that it is God's will to prosper and teach us, that is how we then have faith for giving and receiving. Isaiah 48:17 declares, **"Thus saith the Lord, thy redeemer, the Holy One of Isreal: I am the Lord thy God which TEACHETH THEE TO PROFIT, which leadeth thee by the way that thou shouldest go."** Another translation declares, **"I am the eternal your God, TRAINING YOU for good to PROFIT."** When we yield to the Word of God and obey in tithes and offerings, we become a blessing to the work of God.

God wants us blessed to establish His covenant in the earth. Deuteronomy 8:18 declares, **"But thou shalt remember the Lord thy God: for it is he that GIVETH THEE THE POWER TO OBTAIN WEALTH, that he may ESTABLISH HIS COVENANT which he sware unto thy fathers, as it is this day."** When we tap over into God's method of operation, we will reap the increase, which comes from heaven's influence. The power to obtain wealth is the ability to understand by revelation knowledge how prosperity really works. Once you grab hold of these truths, you will not let a day pass that you will not seek to activate giving to those around you.

He blesses us to be a blessing in life. Genesis 12:2 declares, **"And I will make of thee a great nation, AND I WILL BLESS THEE, and make thy name great; and THOU SHALT BE A BLESSING."** We break loose from financial poverty through our obedience to give unto the

Lord! Lay aside that financial weight and live to give. Learn the rhythm of giving daily unto the Lord, by sowing into the plan of God in the earth. Luke 6:38 declares, **"GIVE AND IT SHALL BE GIVEN UNTO YOU; good measure, pressed down, shaken together, and running over, shall men give into your bosom. For with THE SAME MEASURE THAT YE METE withal it SHALL BE MEASURED TO YOU AGAIN."**

STAY TEACHABLE

It is wise to remain open to instruction from the Lord and others. James 1:19 declares, **"Wherefore, my beloved brethren, let every man be SWIFT TO HEAR, slow to speak, slow to wrath."** The Living Bible Translation is profound, **"Dear brother, don't ever forget that it is best to LISTEN MUCH, speak little and don't become angry."** How many times have we thought we knew it all? Yet, looking back, we saw how wrong our understanding was. What we really needed was to humble ourselves and be willing to grow. It's so easy for human nature to close their ears to good counsel in line with the Word of God. If you think you know it all, you are in a dangerous spiritual condition. Nothing can hinder growth in an individual's life quicker than an unteachable spirit.

Webster's dictionary defines *teachable* as: **one that can be taught, capable of being taught, open to learning and receiving instruction.** One minister put it like this, *"We will never grow into maturity until we have been delivered from a know it all, unteachable spirit."* When we are serving under someone in business or ministry, we must listen and learn, so that we can become all God intends for us. God is always trying to shape us into more. Revival is for those who remain teachable!

AVOID WRONG INFLUENCES

Who and what we allow to influence us is critical. Proverbs 13:20 states, **"He that WALKETH WITH WISE MEN shall be wise: but a companion of fools shall be destroyed."** We cannot fellowship with those who are not living for God, or they will pull us right out of God's will. Look at how wrong influences affected the nation of Israel, **"MY PEOPLE HAVE MINGLED WITH THE HEATHEN AND PICKED UP THEIR**

EVIL WAYS and have become good for nothing" (Hosea 7:8, Living Bible Translation). We cannot mingle with the ungodly and remain godly for very long. We should seek to lead them to Christ, but mingling just to mingle, heads us straight into trouble. Psalm 1:1-2 declares, *"Blessed is the man WALKETH NOT IN THE COUNSEL OF THE UNGODLY, nor sitteth in the seat of the scornful. But his delight is in the law of the Lord; and in his law doth he meditate day and night."*

What about walking with the wise? It is amazing how many of us seek counsel from everyone else except our spiritual leaders. How many times has a true man or woman of God admonished us, only for us to ignore godly counsel? The Apostle Paul experienced the same problem.

On a sea journey to Rome, Paul knew by the Holy Spirit that danger lay ahead. He tried to warn those in charge, only to go unheeded. *"... Sirs, I perceive that this voyage will be with hurt and much damage, not only of the lading and ship, but also of our lives. Nevertheless, the centurion BELIEVED THE MASTER and the OWNER of the ship, more than THOSE THINGS WHICH WERE SPOKEN BY PAUL"* (Acts 27:10-11). The results were devastating. They valued a man of natural experience over a man of spiritual experience. If we read on, we see that God still bailed them out after destruction hit, because they then turned their ear to godly counsel. Amazing, isn't it?

Who are we allowing to influence us? Is it godly or not? Does it line up with God's Word? Are we overriding what God wants for what we want? There are no short cuts to a life of obedience. Determine to take careful inventory of what and who is trying to influence you. Make a straight path to walk with those of like precious faith and company. In Acts 4:1-23, we find Peter and John facing much resistance and threatening for preaching the gospel, *"And being let go, THEY WENT UNTO THEIR OWN COMPANY, and reported all that the chief priests and elders had said unto them."* In times of difficulty there is nothing better than dwelling in the midst of the company of the elect of God.

UNFORGIVENESS

God's forgiveness flows to us in direct proportion to the measure of our forgiveness to our fellowman. Jesus said, *"And when ye stand praying, forgive if ye have ought against any: that your Father also which is in heaven may forgive you your trespasses. But if ye do not forgive, neither will your Father which is in heaven forgive your trespasses"* (Mark 11:25-26). We must forgive and let go of anything that our hearts may be harboring.

Forgiveness is not an emotion; it is an act of the will, an act of obedience to the Lord. Our willingness to forgive keeps us in the peace of God. St Francis of Assisi said, *"It is in pardoning that we are pardoned."* Abraham Lincoln said, *"I am a patient man, always willing to forgive on the Christian terms of repentance, and also to give people ample time for repentance."* Another unknown author said, *"To forgive is to set a prisoner free and discover the prisoner was you."* Don't allow yourself to be hindered from experiencing answered prayer and God's presence by walking in unforgiveness!

Chapter 11

PROPER ATTITUDES TOWARD GODLY LEADERSHIP

"And we beseech you, therefore brethren, to know those who labour among you, and who are over you in the Lord, and admonish you; And to ESTEEM THEM VERY HIGHLY IN LOVE for their WORK'S SAKE. And be at peace among yourselves"
(1 Thessalonians 5:11-12).

"And now, friends, we ask you to HONOR THOSE LEADERS WHO WORK SO HARD FOR YOU, who have been given the responsibility of urging and guiding you along in your obedience. OVERWHELM THEM WITH YOUR APPRECIATION AND LOVE"
(The Message Bible).

"And he gave some APOSTLES; and some PROPHETS; and some EVANGELISTS; And some, PASTORS AND TEACHERS. For the perfecting of the saints, for the work of the ministry, for the edifying of the body of Christ"
(Ephesians 4:11-12).

"Weakness of attitude becomes a weakness of character."
—Albert Einstein

"A positive attitude will have positive results because attitudes are contagious."
—Zig Ziglar

"The only disability in life is a bad attitude."
—Scott Hamilton

It is very evident from the scriptures that God places a great deal of importance on the fivefold ministry gifts in the Body of Christ. Without these God appointed leaders, the body of Christ would never reach full maturity and perfection. Within each fivefold ministry office, there is a special anointing from God to **teach, train, admonish** and **perfect** the body of Christ. While traveling throughout the United States and ministering in many different churches, one thing common in each church congregation is the lack of understanding from the Word of God on how to *show proper respect, relate to* and *honor their pastors*.

The *role of a pastor* is one of the most challenging professions in the world. Pastors are a special breed of individuals, unique and precious in God's sight. Jeremiah 3:15 declares, *"I will GIVE YOU PASTORS according to mine heart, which shall feed you with knowledge and understanding."* When God equips pastors to spiritual leadership, there is an anointing from heaven gracing them to serve and perfect the saints. Until church staffs and members receive pastors as gifts in their lives, learning how to properly relate and treat them, they will miss God and hinder the work of the Lord.

I want to challenge you, as you read this to renew your appreciation for your pastors. Make it a point as the scripture declares to, *"Overwhelm them with your appreciation and love."* The following are *some* biblical principles to follow when relating to your pastor or spiritual leaders.

TREAT THEM WITH HONOR AND RESPECT

In 1 Timothy 5:17, from the God's Word Translation, it declares, *"Give DOUBLE HONOR to SPIRITUAL LEADERS who handle their duties well, this is especially true if they work hard at teaching the word of God."* The Living Bible declares, *"... Pastors who do their work well should be paid well and be HIGHLY APPRECIATED and RESPECTED."* Even though your pastors or leaders are not perfect, we are commanded to show them proper respect and appreciation when relating to them. Don't forget you're not perfect either and should not lose sight of your own areas to grow in the Lord.

The American Heritage Dictionary defines *honor* as: *high respect, to hold in esteem and to show respect for, to show dignity according to a position or to honor an office.* Albert Einstein once said, *"Everyone should be respected as an individual, but no one idolized."* We're not talking about idolizing your pastor or leaders, but maintaining a healthy attitude of respect toward them and the office they stand in and uphold by the grace of God. Romans 13:7, in the Living Bible declares, *"Obey those who are over you and GIVE HONOR and RESPECT to all whom it is due."* The Message Bible declares, *"Fulfill your obligations as a citizen, pay your taxes, RESPECT YOUR LEADERS."*

AVOID THE SIN OF FAMILIARITY

This is a very common occurrence, not only with our pastors and spiritual leaders, but also in our corporate world. I have watched individuals show proper respect for their pastors, and then over a period of time, get to casual and familiar with them and disregard respect for their office. As the old saying goes, *"Familiarity breeds contempt."* Jesus himself had to deal with those who dishonored Him and the calling on His life to be fulfilled.

In Matthew 13:55-57, from the Living Bible we read, *"'How is this possible?' The people exclaimed. 'HE'S JUST THE CARPENTERS SON, and we know Mary his mother and his brothers – James, Joseph, Simon, and Judas. And his sisters-they all live here. HOW CAN HE BE SO GREAT?' And they became angry with him! Then Jesus told them, 'A prophet is HONORED everywhere EXCEPT IN HIS OWN country, AND AMONG HIS OWN PEOPLE. And so he DID ONLY A FEW GREAT MIRACLES THERE, because of their unbelief.'"*

It is obvious from the scriptures that Jesus faced the greatest dishonor among those in his own country. That is so common even in the local church today. The pastor is respected and honored from the Word of God and then over a period of time the staff around him and the congregation get to casual with them and miss God. Have you ever noticed the direct relationship between respect for your pastor and his ability to speak into your life and help you?

Just like Jesus, when the people fell into the sin of familiarity, He did only a few great miracles. In other words, Jesus was limited in His ability to minister to them because they just looked at Him as the carpenter's son. They limited Him by not recognizing Who He was and what God had called Him to do. Until a congregation learns to honor their pastors or appointed leaders, they will never receive from them, missing much blessing from their lives and office. If your pastor seems to have you at arm's length, it may be you are acting *to "buddy, buddy"* instead of showing proper biblical honor.

PRAY FOR THEM

It is a fact, that everyday pastors and spiritual leaders face a great deal of responsibility. They are faced with many spiritual attacks due to the anointing on their lives to lead. They need the wisdom from God and much prayer as they follow God's heart for the ministry and the lives of those around them. It's just so easy to play the *"armchair quarterback,"* when observing their leadership decisions. Instead of using all your energy on pointing out all their shortcomings, why not devote yourself to genuinely pray for them. In 1 Timothy 2:1-3, it declares, **"I exhort therefore, first of all SUPPLICATIONS, PRAYERS, INTERCESSIONS and giving of thanks BE MADE for all men; FOR KINGS and for ALL THAT ARE IN AUTHORITY; that we may lead a quiet and peaceable life in all godliness and honesty. For this is GOOD and ACCEPTABLE in the sight of God our Savior."**

Determine to devote yourselves to pray for your pastors, his family and ministry. God will bless you, and you will maintain the right attitude of heart toward them in the process. It is through your prayers for them that God will show you their hearts anyway.

LEARN TO FOLLOW AND OBEY

I realize when you place your life in the trust of another; there is certain uneasiness; yet the Word of God commands us to be obedient to those in spiritual leadership over us. Hebrews 13:17 from the Young's Translation declares, **"BE OBEDIENT TO THOSE LEADING YOU AND BE SUBJECT, for they do watch for your souls, as about to give account, that they may do it not sighing, for that would be unprofitable to you."** The Living Bible declares, **"Obey your spiritual leaders and be willing** *to do what they say."* Darby's Translation declares, *"**Obey your leaders and be submissive for they watch over your souls as those who shall give account, that they may do it with joy and not groaning.**"*

The Word of God clearly tells us we are to be responsive to our spiritual leaders, following and acting in obedience under their authority. The American Heritage Dictionary defines *obey* as: ***to carry out or to fulfill a command, to carry out an order or instruction given, to behave obediently.*** The true test of submission is to follow when you may not agree with the direction or decisions being made. Please understand, I am not talking about submitting to sin or error. Remember, agreement is easy until you disagree. It is then when the true test of obedience is seen. God asked Abraham to go and take his only son and sacrifice him as and offering. Abraham must have asked himself, *"Is this bad leadership I am under?"* Yet he passed the test in his obedience, and God provide a ram in the bush in place of his son. God proved Abraham's heart to be willing and obedient, a man he could trust and use for his glory. Isaiah 1:19 declares, ***"IF you be WILLING and OBEDIENT, ye shall eat the good of the land."***

In Matthew 8:5-13, we find the centurion soldier requesting help from Jesus concerning his servant who was at home sick of the palsy, grievously tormented. Jesus desired to come and heal his servant and the centurion forbid him to set foot under his roof, requesting Jesus to *"Just speak the word only and my servant will be healed."* Yet, in verse eight we hear the centurion say, ***"FOR I AM A MAN UNDER AUTHORITY, having soldiers under me: and I say to this man, go, and he goeth; and to another, come, and he cometh; and to my servant, Do this, and he doeth it."*** The centurion was labeled by Jesus as having great faith because he understood the relationship between faith and submission. He was a man that personally understood the way authority works. He recognized the power of the word spoken in relationship to the authority.

Determine to trust God and pray for your spiritual leader or pastors and be willing to receive their Godly counsel. Your pastor sees the big picture and many times can't always share the information with you about many matters. Just trust the Lord and follow the counsel of the Word of God from their lives to yours, and God will bless your life dramatically.

BE TEACHABLE

In James 1:19, The Living Bible declares, *"Dear brother, don't ever forget that it is best to LISTEN MUCH, SPEAK LITTLE and DON'T BECOME ANGRY."* The Message Bible declares, *"Post this at all intersections, dear friends LEAD WITH YOUR EARS."* The American Heritage Dictionary defines *teachable* as: *one that can be taught, capable of being taught, a willingness to learn, open to learn and receive instruction*. It's so easy for human nature to close their ears to good counsel in line with the Word of God. If you think you know it all, you are probably in a dangerous place. One minister said it this way, *"get delivered from a know-it-all, unteachable spirit."* Nothing can hinder growth in an individual's life quicker that an unteachable spirit.

Remember, you know all you know, and if you will learn to listen to Godly leadership you can learn so much more. Eric Hoffer said, *"Humility is not the renunciation of pride, but the substitute of one's pride to submit to another's counsel."* Be open to your pastor and spiritual leaders and stay teachable and humble before the Lord, and God will bless your life greatly.

HOOK UP WITH THEIR VISION FROM GOD

Amos 3:3, declares, *"How can two WALK TOGETHER except they BE AGREED."* The New English Bible declares, *"Do men travel together unless they are agreed?"* Your pastors or spiritual leader's vision is the blueprint or goal that God has given them to accomplish for the Kingdom of God. Do all you can to hook up and flow with the vision God has placed in their hearts. Pastors aren't looking for individual members to come into their churches with an agenda and begin to tell the pastor what he should be doing. All good leaders are open to God's ideas; yet they don't want to feel like they are being manipulated to conform to an agenda that God is not leading them to do. The right attitude should always be, *"Pastor you're a man of God, I am here to serve and support the plan that God has for this church or ministry; please tell me how I can best serve you and help you obey God."*

The American Heritage Dictionary defines *agreement* as: *an arrangement between parties regarding a method of action, harmony, to be harmonious, to fit or adept with another.* In 1 Corinthians 1:10 from the Living Bible, it declares, *"But dear brother, I beg you in the name of our lord Jesus Christ stop arguing among yourselves—let there be REAL HARMONY so there won't be splits in the church."* Make a decision that you are going to back leadership and be loyal to support them as they do their best to follow and obey God's mandate upon their lives and ministries.

STAY CLEAR FROM GOSSIP AND STRIFE

Psalm 105:15 declares, *"Saying TOUCH NOT MINE ANOINTED, and do my prophets NO HARM."* The P.K. Harrison Translation reads, *"Leave my anointed ones alone; do not harm my prophets."* Some individuals never realize the dangerous ground they are walking on when they get into opposition with the work of the Lord and hinder God's anointed leaders. When they meddle with their lives, through gossip, strife, and rebellion, they are working harm to them and hindering God's work. The American Heritage Dictionary defines *gossip* as: *spreading rumors or talk, sowing discord, malicious talk, and a person who habitually spreads private rumors.* Gossip is really character assassination. According to the scriptures, gossip and slander are wrong and forbidden by God. Psalm 17:3 declares, *"I have purposed that my mouth shall not transgress."* God has given the gift of speech not to work harm toward his pastors and spiritual leaders, but to pray for and bless them before the eyes of God and man. Repeating leaders faults and weaknesses is idle talk and character assassination that works damage to their reputation.

Satan is called the accuser of the brethren according to Revelations 12:10, thus his desire is to cast a shadow of doubt on his leaders through false accusations. In 1 Timothy 5:19 it declares, *"Against an elder RECEIVE NOT AN ACCUSATION, but before TWO or THREE WITNESSES."* The Weymouth Translation declares, *"NEVER ENTERTAIN AN ACCUSATION against an ELDER ..."* The Beck's Translation declares, *"Don't accept an accusation against a pastor ..."* The Taylor's Translation concludes, *"... unless there are two or three witnesses to accuse him."*

If a pastor is in blatant error, it will be evident to more than one individual and eventually catch up with him anyway. What we all sow in life, we will reap. But for the pastor or spiritual leader who is true, loves God, seeks Him with all his heart to obey God, be careful not to interfere and cause trouble for them. In Galatians 6:17, the Apostle Paul declared, *"From henceforth LET NO MAN TROUBLE ME: for I bear in my body the marks of the Lord Jesus."*

Sure all leaders make some mistakes along the way, just like you, but the Bible tells us that love seeks to cover them. Proverbs 11:13, declares, *"A talebearer revealeth secrets: but he that is of a FAITHFUL SPIRIT CONCEALTH THE MATTER."* With every word of gossip offered against your pastor, you are yielding yourself as a tool of Satan to sow discord among the brethren and discredit them in the eyes of men and women. Proverbs 26:20 declares, *"Where no wood is, there the fire goeth out: so where there is no talebearer, the strife ceases."* Determine right now to stay clear of *controversy, strife and gossip* and *be loyal to support* your pastor or spiritual leader.

BE PATIENT WITH THEM AS THEY ARE WITH YOU

Without a doubt the standards for a Pastor or fivefold ministry gift is high and their responsibilities great. We have to lift the standard high as leaders, as well as the body of Christ. Yet, many times leaders are stepping out to develop and do new things the Lord is directing them with. Be mature enough to know that it will take some time for it to develop and succeed. Don't mistake the pastor's character for a plan that might be developing slowly. Choose always to be a **"green light,"** believe the best and be patient with them as they push forward with the plans of God. Many times when pastors and spiritual leaders are stepping out to do new leading, *"the new leading,"* it may not be perfectly developed yet. Instead of wasting your energy to ride the wave of disbelief, and criticism, be positive, get excited, jump on board and be a part of the answer—not the problem. In 1 Thessalonians 5:14 it declares, *"Now we exhort you brethren, warn them that are unruly, comfort the feebleminded, support the weak, BE PATIENT TOWARD ALL MEN."* The Modern English Translation declares, *"LOSE PATIENCE WITH NONE."* That is a tall order for all of us to continue in and consider.

Maybe your pastor or spiritual leader is growing in an area of their life; do your best to sow the seed of patience, just as they have done with you time and time again, as you have grown spiritually. In 1 Corinthians 13:4-8, we see the great chapter in the Bible to define the qualities of the love of God. The first characteristic mentioned is patience. J.B. Rotherham's Translation of verse 4 declares, *"LOVE IS VERY PATIENT."* The Phillips Translation declares, *"THIS LOVE OF WHICH I SPEAK IS SLOW TO LOSE PATIENCE."* A pastor can do things right a hundred times and miss it once and it's common for people to pounce on the one thing they did wrong, instead of the hundred things that have been done right. Let patience guide you in your overwhelming love for your leaders.

BE RESPECTFUL OF THEIR TIME

It is always the heart of God's pastors to be accessible to people. But they, like you, need special time with their family to rest and have recreation. I have had the honor through the years of traveling and meeting pastors from all over the nations and the majority are *overworked, underpaid, and not appreciated.* In Matthew 8:20, Jesus said, ***"Foxes have holes and birds have nests, but the son of man HAS NO PLACE TO LAY HIS HEAD."*** The Phillips Translation declares, *"… HAS NO PLACE TO CALL HIS OWN."* Like Jesus, pastors are constantly being pulled upon by the needs of people. I think every church board should take up a special offering and send them away free of charge once a year.

If you have to approach your pastor, be sensitive not to do so, two minutes before they have to preach. Maybe you can call his office and set an appointment to meet with them if it's not a *"do or die"* situation. As you continue to grow, you can trust God by going directly to the Word of God and pray for yourself. God will answer and respond to you directly to sustain you in life. Determine to help your pastor or minister with the needs of those under his care, which don't know as much. Luke 6:19 declares, ***"And the whole multitude SOUGHT TO TOUCH HIM: for there went virtue out of him, and he healed them all."*** While the multitudes of individuals are seeking to get your pastors time, determine to help assist them by walking with God for yourself. In doing so, you will help them reach out to those who really do need their time, counsel and ministry.

Chapter 12

LIFTING THE HANDS OF GODLY LEADERS

"And Moses' hands WERE HEAVY; and they took a stone, and put it under him, and he sat thereon; and Aaron and Hur STAYED UP HIS HANDS, the one on the one side, and the other on the other side; and HIS HANDS WERE STEADY until the going down of the sun"
(Exodus 17:12, KJV).

"Moses arms finally become TO TIRED TO HOLD UP THE ROD any longer, so Aaron and Hur rolled a stone for him to sit on, and they stood on each side HOLDING UP HIS HANDS until sunset"
(Exodus 17:12, The Living Bible).

"The servant-leader is servant first. It begins with the natural feeling that one wants to serve, to serve first. Then conscious choice brings one to aspire to lead."
—Woodrow Wilson

"Serving others prepares you to lead others."
—John Ruskin

In Exodus, chapter 17, we read where Moses and all the congregation of Israel suddenly came under attack by Amalek. Moses called Joshua to choose men and go out to fight Amalek the next day. As Joshua fought in the valley below, Moses took Aaron and Hur to the top of the hill to stand with him during the battle.

When Moses held up the rod, Israel prevailed in battle. When Moses' hands got tired and his arms fell, Amalek, the enemy, prevailed. To ensure victory, Aaron and Hur held up the hands of Moses until the end of the battle. As a result, Joshua led the troops of Israel to a major victory, crushing the army of Amalek by the sword. (Exodus 17:8-13). Praise the Lord!

THE MINISTRY OF HELPS

We must never underestimate how important it is to support our pastors and *lift up the hands* of the fivefold leaders in these last days. Ministry is not an easy work. It demands much from its spiritual leaders.

The Lord designed the fivefold ministry gifts to lead the body of Christ into maturity. Ephesians 4:11-12 declares, ***"And he gave some, apostles; and some prophets; and some, evangelists; and pastors and teachers; For the perfecting of the saints, for the work of the ministry, for the edifying of the body of Christ."*** We must do all we can to *be a strong support* to the local church and to get behind our pastors with prayer and deed.

Just as Aaron and Hur were called alongside of Moses, God has called men and women to *lift up the hands* of pastors and other fivefold ministries as they carry out God's will in the earth. In 1 Corinthians 12:27-28, the Apostle Paul defines that role as "helps." ***"Now are ye the body of Christ And members in particular. And God hath set some in the church, first apostles, secondarily prophets, thirdly teachers, after that miracles, then gifts of healings, HELPS, governments, diversities of tongues."*** Here, two ministry gifts are named that were not mentioned in Ephesians 4:11: helps and diversity of tongues.

We don't hear much spoken about the ministry of helps; yet, it is vital to the success of the ministry. Without it the fivefold ministry gifts would not be able to attend to prayer and the teaching and preaching of God's Word. George Whitfield once said, ***"I am tired in the Lord's work, but not tired of it."*** The facts are simple, pastors and fivefold ministry gifts carry an awesome responsibility and they can grow tired in the battle.

BECOMING PROFITABLE TO YOUR PASTOR

As I travel around the country, I see many outstanding pastors over worked, under paid, not appreciated and desperate to find people they can trust to help them obey God. The scriptures teach that some are called by grace to a ministry of helps. But all are called to be helpful.

In 2 Timothy 4:11, we find an example of Mark and his supportive role to the Apostle Paul. ***"Only Luke is with me, take MARK and bring him with thee: FOR HE IS PROFITABLE TO ME FOR THE MINISTRY."*** The NIV declares, ***"... For he is HELPFUL TO ME in MY MINISTRY."***

You might say, *"I am not called to the ministry of helps."* Even so, you can still stand behind your pastors. Be faithful in prayer, tithing, church attendance and church vision. Your supportive attitude will help lift their hands.

BRING REFRESHING TO YOUR PASTOR

God calls us to be a blessing to all people, especially those who devote themselves to lead us in the faith. In 2 Timothy 1:16-17 we find another example of an individual used by God to bring support to the Apostle Paul. ***"The Lord give mercy to the house of On-e-siph-orus, FOR HE HAS OFTEN REFRESHED ME, and was not ashamed of my chains. But when he was in Rome, he SOUGHT ME OUT VERY DILIGENTLY and found me."***

Here we see a man inspired by God to seek out the man of God to *refresh him.* What an outstanding example of blessing leadership instead of causing trouble for them. The Amplified Bible declares, ***"... For he hath OFTEN SHOWED ME KINDNESS AND MINISTERED TO MY NEEDS—comforting and reviving and bracing me like fresh air."*** The Taylor's Translation declares, ***"His visits REVIVED ME like a BREATH OF FRESH AIR."*** The New English Bible declares, ***"He relieved me in my troubles."***

What could be said of us? *Are we a breath of fresh air, a relief and a comfort for leadership?* Determine to do so, and God will richly bless you and your family.

PART OF THE ANSWER NOT THE PROBLEM

Look for ways to be a blessing and encouragement to your pastors. Don't fault find or hurt them with unloving actions. Give yourself to pray for them. Believe God's best about and for them. True pastors are sincere and want to see people know God and live for Him.

Helpers bring change for the better. Don't be a troublemaker for your pastor. We can be a huge help or hindrance. Look at 2 Timothy 4:14, *"Alexander the coppersmith did me MUCH EVIL: the Lord shall reward him according to his works."* The Amplified declares, *"Alexander the coppersmith did me <u>GREAT WRONGS</u>. The Lord will PAY HIM BACK FOR HIS ACTIONS."*

Most people, who cause trouble for godly leaders, fail to see that they will be paid back for working hurt and trouble. They will reap the seeds they have sown! David said in Psalm 105:15, *"Saying, TOUCH NOT GOD'S ANOINTED and do my prophets NO HARM."* The Message Bible declares, *"Don't you dare lay a hand on my anointed, don't hurt a hair on the heads of my prophets."*

Does it sound like God thinks a lot about His ministers? He will defend them against those who work harm and bring wrong to their lives. The P.K. Harrison Translation is just as strong, *"Leave my anointed ones alone; and do not harm my prophets."*

You might say, "Alexander the coppersmith wasn't a Christian." You are right! You can expect such behavior from a person who doesn't have Jesus Christ and His love nature. What's sad is when Christians who know God and should walk in love, bring hurt to a godly, anointed pastor or leader and think nothing of it. This happens too often because of immaturity—no fear of the Lord or a lack of respect for healthy, godly authority.

SIN NOT AGAINST YOUR PASTOR

You might say, *"But Dr. Chris, my pastors have made all kinds of mistakes. Their leadership needs improving."* Question: *Haven't you also made mistakes? Don't you also need improving?*

Remember David, who authored *"touch not mine anointed,"* served under a mad King. King Saul was jealous of David and wanted to kill him. King Saul attempted to kill David twenty-one times.

Yet, David behaved himself wisely and did not retaliate against an **extreme case of bad leadership**. He left judgment in the hands of God. David had a right to strike back at Saul in defense, but he simply would not. Even when he just cut a small piece of King Saul's skirt, he repented.

"And David said to Saul, 'Wherefore hearest thou men's words, saying, 'Behold David seeketh thy hurt?' Behold this day thine eyes have seen how the Lord had delivered thee today into mine hand in the cave: and some bade me kill thee; and I said, 'I WILL NOT PUT FORTH MINE HAND AGAINST MY lord; FOR HE IS THE LORD'S ANOINTED.' Moreover, my father, see, yea, see the skirt of thy robe in my hand: for I cut off the skirt of thy robe in my hand: for in that I cut off the skirt of thy robe, and killed thee not, know thou see that there is neither evil nor transgression in mine hand, and I HAVE NOT SINNED AGAINST THEE; yet thou huntest my soul to take" (1 Samuel 24:9-11).

Chances are very high that your pastors are not attempting to throw spears in your direction to kill you, like Saul did to David. If they are, I suggest you go online to find a new church! The point I want to get to you is this: look at David's extreme case and how he still chose not to sin against leadership. He waited for God to move.

Do likewise with the wonderful pastors you have. Keep your hands and mouths off of them. Instead, lift up their hands. Help them fulfill God's supernatural plan for your city or community. They need your help in whatever capacity God has graced you with. Be patient and sow mercy toward their lives as they seek to follow God's plan.

Look for ways to refresh, bless and encourage your pastors. They are not perfect, but neither are you, so work together with a humble spirit and help them impact the world.

PRAY FOR YOUR PASTOR

In 1 Timothy 2:1-3, the Apostle Paul exhorts us to pray for all those who are in authority, *"I exhort therefore, that first of all, supplications, **PRAYERS, INTERCESSIONS**, and giving of thanks, be made FOR ALL MEN; for kings and **ALL THAT ARE IN AUTHORITY**; that we may lead a quiet and peaceable life in all godliness and honesty. For this IS GOOD and ACCEPTABLE in the SIGHT OF GOD OUR SAVIOR."*

According to this portion of scripture, prayers and intercessions for all in authority is good and acceptable in God's sight. When He declares we ought to pray for all in authority, does that mean your pastors also? The answer is simple, of course! One way and a very important way you can hold up the hands of your pastors or leaders is to regularly pray for them.

We have several board members with our ministry, and we appreciate them all very much. There is one special couple that I speak with often that mention they are actively praying for our special meetings as I travel. They know our schedule and pray for me and the special services. This means the world to me. When I am out on the front battle lines, contending for lives to be changed by God's Word and His anointing, it's good to know others are praying for us. Your pastors need prayer, too.

Be an Aaron and a Hur. Be of the caliber of David. Lift the hands of your pastors in prayer. It will give God a chance to knit your hearts together.

James 5:16 declares, ***"... The EFFECTUAL, FERVANT PRAYER OF A RIGHTEOUS MAN AVAILETH MUCH."***

Chapter 13

CONTENDING FOR HIS PRESENCE

"You are the God who performs miracles; you display your power among the people"
(Psalm 77:14, NIV).

"Ye men of Israel, hear these words; Jesus of Nazareth, a man approved of God among you by miracles and wonders and signs, which God did by him in the midst of you, as ye yourselves also know:"
(Acts 2:22).

"The purpose of the spirited filled life is to demonstrate the supernatural power of the living God so that the unsaved multitudes will abandon their dead gods to call on the name of the Lord and be delivered."
—T.L. Osborn

"A church in the land without the power of God is a curse, rather than a blessings."
—D.L. Moody

The Early Church constantly witnessed God's supernatural power. Every time the good news of Jesus was preached, the atmosphere was ignited with the miraculous. Blind eyes and deaf ears were opened, the dead were raised, the lame walked and masses of people believed on Jesus as a result. The supernatural power of God demonstrated the authenticity of the message.

The Apostle Paul described it this way in 1 Corinthians 2:4-5, **"And my speech and my preaching was not with enticing words of man's wisdom, BUT IN DEMONSTRATION OF THE SPIRIT AND OF POWER: That your faith should not stand in the wisdom of men, but** *in the power of God."* Then in Hebrews 2:3-4, *"How shall we escape if we neglect so great salvation; which at the first began to be spoken by the Lord, and was CONFIRMED unto us by them that heard Him; God also bearing them witness, both with SIGNS AND WONDERS, AND DIVERS MIRACLES, AND GIFTS OF THE HOLY GHOST, according to his own will?"*

What about today? Where has the Church's passion gone for the supernatural works of God in our midst? Have we become so comfortable that we no longer hunger for the glory and power of God?

Yes, there are waves of God's glory sweeping the earth. It has been this way with every generation. But what about our own hearts—is it sweeping there, too? Numbers 14:21 says**,** ***"But as truly as I live, all the earth shall be FILLED WITH THE GLORY OF THE LORD."*** We have been called to carry the anointing of God to teach and preach the gospel and display the miraculous in His name. (Matthew 9:35, Acts 10:38, Colossians 1:18).

And, yes, we are in the last days, which will be the Church's most glorious hour. But just when we should be moving forward with signs, wonders and miracles—the display of the miraculous—many ministries appear to be backing off. We have seen the Gospel subtly watered down and the supernatural tucked away because we're too sophisticated for all that! Or it has been so long since it has been among us that we stopped expecting God to show up in glorious ways?

But God ... there is the end of the argument right there. But God ... did He change? Hebrews 13:8 states, ***"Jesus Christ the same yesterday, and today, and forever."*** But God ... has He lost interest? But God ... what about His plan? But God is raising up a remnant of believers who will not back down, who will not shut up and who will not stop contending for the supernatural.

Without the manifested presence of God demonstrated among us, we carry an impotent message. What distinguishes the message of Christ from any other? It is the evidence that follows—*the power, the wonders, the miracles*. These demonstrate that there is One Higher and Greater among us and in us. (1 John 4:4).

God is not ashamed of Who He is. Are we? Are we willing to risk offending some in order that the power of God might flow through us to rescue the afflicted, the hurting, and the lost? It does not come without a cost. Jesus said, *"If any man will come after Me, let him deny himself, and take up his cross daily and follow Me"* (Luke 9:23). It costs us the comfortable; it requires intense dedication and fervor for the will of God.

In the last days many will turn their backs on the power of God, refusing to allow the Holy Spirit to manifest in their midst. The Apostle Paul warned us in 2 Timothy 3:5, *"Having a form of godliness, but denying the power thereof: from such turn away."*

Some other translations say:
"They will maintain a facade of religion" —Phillips
"They will go to church yes, but deny the power" —Taylor's
"But not giving expression to its power" —William's
"But refuse to let it be a power" —Goodspeed
"They will turn their backs on the power" —Basic English
"They are strangers to the power" —Berkley's
"They are standing in denial of its reality" —New English
"They will make a show of religion, but behind the scenes they are animals" —The Message Bible

We are all called to flow in the supernatural power of the Spirit of God. Here are some biblical principles from the Word of God that will help us position ourselves to contend for the supernatural.

APPETITE FOR GOD

John G. Lake once said, *"There is a certain spirit of desperation that accompanies hunger. I wish we all had it spiritually. I wish we were desperately hungry for God. Wouldn't it be glorious?"* The bottom line is that when we become hungry for God, we will have Him moving in our lives. Jesus said, *"Blessed are they which do hunger and thirst after righteousness: for they shall be filled"* (Matthew 5:6). The Message Bible declares, *"You're blessed when you've worked up a good appetite for God. His food and drink is the best meal you'll ever eat."*

We have misplaced our God-given appetites for His presence and a display of the supernatural, trying to pacify them with the carnal. We were created to be fulfilled by the loving presence of a very supernatural God. (Philippians 3:10; Colossians 3:1-2, 5; Psalm 42:1-2).

King David longed to walk with God—it was his passion and hunger. Listen to his heart cry out, *"O God, thou art my God; early will I SEEK THEE: MY SOUL THIRSTETH FOR THEE, MY FLESH LONGETH FOR THEE in a dry and thirsty land, where no water is. To SEE THY POWER and THY GLORY, so as I have seen thee in the sanctuary"* (Psalm 63:1-2). When David says he thirsts for God like water, he is describing his longing for the presence of God.

Our level of hunger will determine our fullness of God and the supernatural flow of His glory in our lives.

A MESSAGE OF FAITH

We cannot expect faith to rise in the hearts of others without the message of Christ being preached. (Romans 10:17; Romans 1:16-17). Jesus said, *"Man shall not live by bread alone, but by every word that proceedeth out of the mouth of God"* (Matthew 4:4).

We must stay with the purity of the Word of God. Watering down the message with our own interpretations and opinions will not help anyone. **God will back up and confirm <u>His Word</u> with signs following!** Results come as we embrace the truth and confess it as our reality. (John 8:32; John 15:7; Proverbs 11:9).

John G. Lake believed that there were three things that contributed to a strong, healthy Christian life:
1) A good confession of one's faith to others
2) A constant prayer life
3) A constant feeding, reading and studying of the Word of God

The Word of God is key to the power of God. Romans 1:16 says, *"For I am not ashamed of the gospel of Christ: for it is THE POWER OF GOD UNTO SALVATION to everyone that believeth."* Hebrews 4:12 says, *"THE WORD OF GOD IS QUICK AND POWERFUL."* In Acts 19, the supernatural power of God caused a revival to break out. The entire region was changed as the name of the Lord was glorified among the Jews and Greeks. It was so powerful that even those practicing magic repented and burned their books, which were full of lies contrary to the Word of God. The Word of God took preeminence. *"SO MIGHTILY*

GREW THE WORD OF GOD AND PREVAILED" (Acts 19:20).

We must keep ourselves continually built up upon God's Word, keeping our faith strong in the power of God. Let's saturate ourselves in His Word, teaching and preaching the message of power and freedom by the inspiration of the Holy Spirit. Colossians 4:6 declares, ***"Let your speech be always with grace, seasoned with salt, that ye may know how ye ought to answer every man."***

TOTAL DEDICATION TO GOD

We will miss the supernatural power of God when our commitment is lacking. God is looking for whole-hearted commitment, complete dedication. Remember Jesus said, ***"If a man will come after Me, let him deny himself and take up his cross daily and follow Me"*** (Luke 9:23). The Phillips Translation says, ***"He must give up all rights to himself."*** And the Message Bible says, ***"Anyone who intends to come with Me has to let me lead. You're not in the drivers seat, I am."***

We need to surrender self-will and be God-willed. (Hebrews 11:6). We are spirit, soul, and body, and God requires Lordship over every area. We are taught in Deuteronomy 6:5, ***"And thou shalt love the Lord thy God with all THINE HEART, and with ALL THY SOUL, and with ALL THY MIGHT."*** It is in this place of crucifixion of self and surrender to God that His supernatural influence moves through our lives.

In Luke 22:42, Jesus prayed, ***"Father, if Thou be willing, remove this cup from me: nevertheless, not My will but Thine be done."*** The Message Bible declares, ***"Please, not what I want, what do you want?"*** Our hearts should also cry, *"Lord, only what you desire for my life!"*

PURITY

John G. Lake once said, ***"A holy God needs holy vessels to flow through."*** God still demands clean living before heaven and man. Hebrews 12:14 makes it clear that holiness and God's presence go hand in hand, ***"Follow after peace with all men and holiness without which no man shall see the Lord."*** The Goodspeed Translation declares, ***"Strive for a HOLY LIFE, CONSECRATED, without which no man shall see the Lord."***

Smith Wigglesworth made this profound statement, *"**Worldliness is that which dulls my affections toward God**"* (see 2 Corinthians 6:14-16). We are full of something, either God or the world. The Lord wants us to set our affections upon Him so that His presence and power can be at work in us. Holiness is an open invitation for the Holy Spirit to move among us.

Let's read Psalm 24:3-4, **"*Who shall ascend into the hill of the Lord? Or who shall stand in His holy place? He that hath clean hands and a pure heart; who hath not lifted up his soul unto vanity; nor sworn deceitfully.*"** Jesus said, **"*Blessed are the pure in heart: for they shall see God*"** (Matthew 5:8). The New English Bible declares, **"*Blessed are the clean in heart for they shall see God.*"** Let's continue to yield to the Lord as He works what is pleasing to Him on the inside of us.

PRAYING IN THE SPIRIT

The subject of prayer can be taken down many roads. But the major key is that it produces great power in the lives of believers. We are encouraged in the Word to pray in the Spirit, **"*PRAYING ALWAYS with all prayer and supplication IN THE SPIRIT, and watching thereunto with all perseverance and supplication for all saints*"** (Ephesians 6:18). Praying in the Spirit is a doorway for the supernatural to work in our lives. We build ourselves up, and we sharpen ourselves to hear the voice of God. (Romans 8:14-16; 26-28).

Jude 1:20 says, **"*But ye, beloved, building up yourselves on your most holy faith, PRAYING IN THE HOLY GHOST.*"** The Living Bible declares, *"... learn to pray in the power and strength of the Holy Spirit."*

John G. Lake said that it was the baptism of the Holy Spirit that made the difference in His ministry. He also said, *"I don't like to get into extremes, but when it comes to speaking in tongues I don't mind."* When we speak in tongues, we edify ourselves. (1 Corinthians 14:4).

Praying in the Spirit positions us to be used in the supernatural. The Apostle Paul, whose ministry was marked by signs and wonders, said, *"I thank my God, I speak with tongues more than ye all"* (1 Corinthians 14:18). He knew the power available and tapped into the supernatural by praying in the Spirit.

When we choose to take the time we have such joy awaiting us in the place of prayer. In 2 Corinthians 13:14, it declares, *"The amazing grace of the Master Jesus Christ, the extravagant love of God, the INTIMATE FRIENDSHIP of the HOLY SPIRIT be with all of you"* (The Message Bible). There remains an intimate friendship with the Holy Spirit for us, where He reveals to us and through us the depths of God.

A SERVANT'S HEART

Why would God be willing to place His glory and power in "earthen vessels?" Because those who truly yield to His will, He equips to carry it out. We have a job to do: we must lift up the name of Jesus so that those in darkness can come to His light.

Jesus did not serve Himself while on this earth. He became the ultimate servant of God and mankind and stripped the devil of his authority and power over us. He set Himself aside to promote life and freedom for us!

The message of the world is to serve, promote, and look after yourself first! But the message of Jesus is to set yourself aside and promote the progress of others in their faith in Christ. We become a channel of God's love and power, flowing out to others.

Jesus chose to set aside His mighty deity and power and humble himself as a man. *"But made Himself of no reputation and took upon Him the form of a servant, and was made in the likeness of men: And being found in fashion as a man, He humbled Himself, and became obedient unto death, even the death of the cross"* (Philippians 2:7-8). His obedience led to His glorification. God has given Him the name above every name. Even when man dishonors us, God will place His honor upon us when we esteem His will over our own.

The anointing rests upon those with a heart for service, service to the will of God, which is always reaching people with the message of Christ. Albert Einstein once said, *"Only a life lived for others is a life worth living."* And Lord Halifax said, *"Service is the rent we pay for our room and board in the earth."*

What can we do to encourage, promote, and lift up those around us? Step out and help others toward Jesus and watch the supernatural flow!

ABOUT THE AUTHOR

Dr. Christopher Mark D'Amico is the president and founder of CDM International of Sarasota, Florida. He is a 1985 graduate of the University of Buffalo, where he graduated with a B.S. in Business Management.

While at the University, he was a four-year-starter as a wide receiver for the UB Bulls football team. Over his four year career, he broke seven school records, was elected first team All ECAC in his junior and senior year as a wide receiver. He was also elected All-American in the wide receiver position. In 1984, he was awarded the honor of Male Athlete of the year by the Police Athletic League. In 2001, he was inducted into the Hall of Fame at the University of Buffalo for his career accomplishments. Upon graduation he had three professional football invitations from the Buffalo Bills, Dallas Cowboys and Tampa Bay Buccaneers.

Turning down the professional invitations, he felt the call of God to public service. He then attended Rhema Bible College in Broken Arrow, Oklahoma, under the leadership of Kenneth Hagin, graduating in 1987. After graduating from Bible College, Dr. Chris served faithfully over eight years in the local church in associate roles in three different states in the USA.

His work experience ranged from youth ministry to young adults, associate work and the academic dean of Texas Bible College in Columbus, Texas. He later moved to Tulsa, Oklahoma, and incorporated Chris D'Amico Ministries. Then he began traveling to over 30 states in the USA and now to many nation of the world in person and by way of special zoom meetings.

In conjunction with his traveling ministry, Dr. Chris served honorably for the Kenneth Hagin Ministries Healing School.

In June of 2021, Dr. Chris received an honorary doctorate from Life Christian University in Tampa, Florida.

Now based and located in Sarasota, Florida, Dr. Chris continues to travel the nation and the world, contending for the uncompromising Word of God, as well as contending for the supernatural power of God to his generation!

To contact Dr. Chris go to:
www.chrisdamicoministries.com
email: chrisdamico75@gmail.com
or call: 941-600-2114

www.ingramcontent.com/pod-product-compliance
Lightning Source LLC
Chambersburg PA
CBHW071215160426
43196CB00012B/2313